EUROPEAN JOURNAL OF WORK AND ORGANIZATIONAL PSYCHOLOGY

Editor
Fred Zijlstra, Department of Psychology, School of Human Sciences,
University of Surrey, Guildford, Surrey GU2 5XH, UK. Email: F.zijlstra@surrey.ac.uk

Associate Editors
Christian Dormann, Arbeits-, Organisations- und Wirtschaftpsychologie,
Johannes Gutenberg-Universität Mainz, Germany

José Maria Peiró, Faculdad de Psicología, Universidad de Valencia, Spain

Michael West, Aston Business School, Aston University, Birmingham, UK

Book Reviews Editor
Robert A. Roe, Universiteit Maastricht, Department of
Organization Studies, P.O. Box 616, 6200 MD Maastricht, The Netherlands

Editorial Board

European Journal of Work and Organizational Psychology is published by Psychology Press Ltd, a member of the Taylor & Francis Group. Correspondence for the publisher should be addressed to *European Journal of Work and Organizational Psychology*, Psychology Press Ltd, 27 Church Road, Hove, East Sussex BN3 2FA, UK.

Information about Psychology Press journals and other publications is available from http://www.psypress.co.uk. Go to http://www.tandf.co.uk/journals/pp/1359432X.html for current information about this journal, including how to access the online version or to register for the free table of contents alerting service.

Subscription rates to Volume 14, 2005 (4 issues) are as follows:
To individuals: UK: £140.00 • Rest of world: $231.00
To institutions: UK: £304.00 • Rest of world: $502.00
Members of the European Association of Work and Organizational Psychology (EAWOP) receive the journal as part of their membership package. Membership enquiries for EAWOP should be sent to cgoffinet@ulg.ac.be, and further information about EAWOP can be obtained from http://www.eawop.org/. Members of the International Association of Applied Psychology (IAAP) qualify for a reduced subscription rate – please contact customer services (see address below) for details.

New subscriptions and changes of address should be sent to Customer Services, Psychology Press, c/o Taylor & Francis Ltd., Rankine Road, Basingstoke, Hampshire RG24 8PR, UK (fax: +44 (0) 1256 330245; email: journal.orders@tandf.co.uk). Please send change of address notices at least six weeks in advance, and include both old and new addresses.

European Journal of Work and Organizational Psychology **(USPS permit number 021134)** is published quarterly in March, June, September, and December. The 2005 US Institutional subscription price is $502.00. Periodicals postage paid at Champlain, NY, by US Mail Agent IMS of New York, 100 Walnut Street, Champlain, NY. **US Postmaster**: Please send address changes to pEWO, PO Box 1518, Champlain, NY 12919, USA.

European Journal of Work and Organizational Psychology is covered by the following indexing/abstracting services: Ergonomics Abstracts; Sociological Abstracts; Social Services Abstracts; Social Sciences Citation Index; Current Contents/Social & Behavioral Sciences; Psychological Abstracts/PsycINFO.

Typeset by Elite Typesetting Techniques Ltd., Eastleigh, Hampshire, UK

T0316327

Aims and scope

The *European Journal of Work and Organizational Psychology* aims to bring together practitioners and academics from all areas of the discipline, and to stimulate the exchange of ideas, opinions and thoughts between these groups. The journal publishes empirical, theoretical and review articles of high scientific quality that are relevant to the real-world situations faced by professionals.

The journal fosters European research, but is not exclusively European, having an international authorship, readership and editorial board. Submissions from all around the world are invited.

The journal primarily publishes freely submitted contributions, but will occasionally also publish a themed issue, although all contributions are submitted to rigorous peer review. Papers and themed issues are published on a wide range of topics covered by the umbrella of work, organizational, industrial and occupational psychology. These include organizational change, organizational climate, team work, motivation, innovation, leadership, bullying, stress in the workplace, burnout, job satisfaction, job design, selection and training.

Submission of manuscripts

Manuscripts are invited for submission. Please note that authors are encouraged to submit papers electronically to expedite the peer review process. Please email your paper, saved in a standard document format type such as Word, Rich Text Format, or PDF, to **reviews@psypress.co.uk** Alternatively, if you wish to submit a hard copy, please send one copy of the manuscript AND a disk version to: Journals Editorial Assistant, Psychology Press Ltd, 27 Church Road, Hove, East Sussex, BN3 2FA, UK. Tel: (0)1273 225007; Fax: (0)1273 205612.

Your covering email/letter must include full contact details (including email), the title of the journal to which you are submitting, and the title of your article.

All manuscripts should be submitted in American Psychological Association (APA) format following the latest edition of *Publication Manual of the APA* (currently 5th edition).

Full instructions for authors are available on the journal website at:
www.tandf.co.uk/journals/pp/1359432X.html

Copyright

It is a condition of publication that authors vest copyright in their articles, including abstracts, in Psychology Press Ltd. This enables us to ensure full copyright protection and to disseminate the article, and the journal, to the widest possible readership in print and electronic formats as appropriate. Authors may, of course, use the material elsewhere after publication providing that prior permission is obtained from Psychology Press Ltd. Authors are themselves responsible for obtaining permission to reproduce copyright material from other sources. To view the 'Copyright Transfer Frequently Asked Questions' please visit http://www.tandf.co.uk/journals/copyright.asp

Back issues

Taylor & Francis retains a 3-year back issue stock of journals. Older volumes are held by our official stockists: Periodicals Service Company, 11 Main Street, Germantown, NY 12526, USA to whom all orders and enquiries should be addressed. Tel: +1 518 537 4700; Fax: +1 518 537 5899; Email: psc@periodicals.com; URL: http://www. periodicals.com/tandf.html

EUROPEAN JOURNAL OF WORK AND
ORGANIZATIONAL PSYCHOLOGY
2005, 14 (2), 105–117

Conflict in organizations: Beyond effectiveness and performance

Carsten K. W. De Dreu and Bianca Beersma

University of Amsterdam, The Netherlands

Conflict theory and research has traditionally focused on conflict management strategies, in relation to individual and work-team effectiveness and productivity. Far less attention has been devoted to "soft" outcomes including job satisfaction, organizational commitment, turnover intentions, and individual health and well-being. This state of affairs is unfortunate because it isolates conflict theory and research from broader issues in organizational psychology and organizational behaviour research. It also impedes applied work in that it remains uncertain how interventions influence not only conflict and effectiveness, but also satisfaction and well-being. This introductory article deals with these problems in detail. The articles in this Special Issue each in their own way deal with one of these issues in more depth, shedding light on how conflict theory and research can be connected to organizational psychology in general.

Although the importance of conflict at work is difficult to underestimate, our knowledge about the effects organizational conflict can have is relatively limited and narrow. Much effort has gone into understanding the ways employees and supervisors manage conflict at work, and many studies have been conducted to decipher the intricacies of conflict and negotiation processes in both the social psychological laboratory and within work teams in organizations. Over the past 20 years an increasing number of studies have considered the possible consequences conflict in work teams has on individual and work-team effectiveness and productivity, showing that under specific circumstances conflict at work can even be functional and result in increased performance (De Dreu, Harinck, & Van Vianen, 1999; Thomas, 1992; Tjosvold, 1998).

Correspondence should be addressed to Carsten K. W. de Dreu, University of Amsterdam, Department of Psychology, Roetersstraat 15, 1018 WB Amsterdam, The Netherlands. Email: c.k.w.dedreu@uva.nl

Our work has been facilitated by grant NWO 410-21-013 of the Dutch Science Foundation awarded to Carsten K. W. de Dreu. We are grateful to Ellen Giebels, Andreas Richter, and Francesco Medina for comments on a previous version of this article.

http://www.tandf.co.uk/journals/pp/1359432X.html   DOI: 10.1080/13594320444000227

These developments have, however, also resulted in a rather one-sided understanding of the consequences organizational conflict can have. Although by now we have a fairly well-developed and researched understanding of conflict management and its effects on productivity, far less attention has been devoted to "soft" outcomes including job satisfaction, organizational commitment, turnover intentions, and individual health and well-being. This state of affairs is unfortunate because it isolates conflict theory and research from broader issues in organizational psychology and organizational behaviour research. It is also unfortunate because it impedes applied work in that it remains uncertain how interventions influence not only conflict and effectiveness, but also satisfaction and well-being. Practitioners may feel uncomfortable with proposed interventions because raising performance through conflict stimulation (for examples, see Van de Vliert, 1997) could simultaneously lower job satisfaction and organizational commitment, and thus inadvertently stimulate absenteeism and involuntary turnover, and stimulate deviant workplace behaviours including sabotage and bullying (Robinson & Bennett, 1995).

In this article we do three things. First, we briefly review the insights about conflict that conflict management research and theory have revealed thus far. Second, and more importantly, we provide an overview of the variables and processes that are key in organizational psychology yet isolated from conflict theory and research. Third, we briefly introduce the four articles that follow this introductory article and that each in their own way try to redress the problems noted above. Together, this set of studies provides a first step towards a more integrated theory about organizational conflict.

STATE OF THE ART: MANAGING CONFLICT TO SECURE EFFECTIVE WORK

Although a myriad of definitions have been suggested, organizational psychologists more and more agree that conflict is best viewed as a process that begins when an individual or group perceives differences and opposition between him- or herself and another individual or group about interests, beliefs, or values that matter to him or her (De Dreu et al., 1999; Wall & Callister, 1995). Perceived differences and opposition evolve around work- and task-related issues, or around socioemotional and relationship issues (e.g., Amason, 1996; Jehn, 1995). Task conflicts involve disputes about the distribution and allocation of resources, opposed views with regard to the procedures and policies that should be used or adhered to, or disagreeing judgements and interpretations of facts. Relationship conflicts involve irritation about personal taste and interpersonal style, disagreements about political preferences, or opposing values (De Dreu & Van de Vliert, 1997).

CONFLICT MANAGEMENT

The ways people manage their conflicts can be infinite. Research and theory converges on the taxonomy advanced in Blake and Mouton's (1964) Conflict Management Grid, and its close cousin Dual Concern Theory (Pruitt & Rubin, 1986; see also Thomas, 1992). Although labelling differs across theories, four different ways of managing conflict are distinguished—contending (or forcing), conceding (or yielding), avoiding (comprising inaction and withdrawing), and collaborating (or problem solving). Contending—trying to impose one's will onto the other side—involves threats and bluffs, persuasive arguments, and positional commitments. Conceding, which is oriented towards accepting and incorporating the other's will, involves unilateral concessions, unconditional promises, and offering help. Avoiding, which involves a passive stance, is aimed at reducing and downplaying the importance of the conflict issues, and at suppressing thinking about them. Collaborating, finally, is oriented towards achieving an agreement that satisfies both one's own and the other's aspirations as much as possible, and involves an exchange of information about priorities and preferences, showing insights, and making tradeoffs between important and unimportant issues.

Which strategy an individual adopts depends on his or her low or high concern for self combined with his or her high or low concern for other. Again, the labels for these two dimensions vary: Concern for self is sometimes labelled "resistance to concession making" (Carnevale & Pruitt, 1992), "concern for the task" (Blake & Mouton, 1964), or "assertiveness" (Thomas, 1992). Sometimes, concern for other is labelled "concern for people" (Blake & Mouton, 1964), or "cooperativeness" (Thomas, 1992). The specific labels used, or the specific ways these dimensions are operationalized, does not seem to influence their effects (De Dreu, Weingart, & Kwon, 2000). What remains is that the specific combination of concern for self, and for other, determines the conflict management strategies adopted. Thus, avoiding results from low dual concern whereas collaborating results from high dual concern. Contending results from high concern for self, and low concern for other, whereas conceding results from low concern for self combined with high concern for other.

Self-concern and other-concern are predicted by one's personality and the situation (De Dreu et al., 2000; Pruitt & Rubin, 1986; Van de Vliert, 1997). Traits influencing these dimensions include social value orientation, power motivation, and need for affiliation. States affecting self- and other-concern derive from incentives, instructional primes, time pressures, level of aspiration, and power preponderance. Reviewing these traits and states is beyond the scope of the current presentation (see De Dreu & Carnevale, 2003; Pruitt, 1998; Van de Vliert, 1997). What is important is that self-concern and other-concern derive from both the person and the situation, and that conflict management strategies thus derive from both the person and the situation. Conflict management, therefore, is not simply a personality characteristic.

INDIVIDUAL AND WORK GROUP EFFECTIVENESS

Apart from analysing the (origins of the) ways employees manage conflict at work, conflict researchers have examined the possible effects conflict has on individual and work-team effectiveness and productivity. Two perspectives surface in the literature—an information-processing perspective, and a conflict typology framework.

According to the *information-processing perspective*, conflict has an inverted U-shape relationship with cognitive flexibility, creative thinking, and problem-solving capacities. This perspective is based on Yerkes and Dodson's (1908) classic demonstration of an inverted U-shaped relation between need level and task achievement, and the idea that some stress is better for task performance than no stress or (too) high levels of stress (Broadbent, 1972). Walton (1969) likewise argued that at low tension levels, conflict leads to inactivity and avoidance, neglect of information, and low joint performance. At high tension levels, it reduces the capacity to perceive, process, and evaluate information. At moderate tension levels, however, conflict parties will seek and integrate information, consider more alternatives, and experience a strong impulse to improve the situation.

The information-processing perspective thus implies that the relationship between conflict and information processing is curvilinear so that performance benefits from moderate levels of conflict, but not from either low or high levels of conflict. Compared to low levels of conflict, moderate levels arouse employees to consider and scrutinize the problem at hand, to generate ideas, and to select and implement adequate problem solutions. At higher levels of conflict, however, the high amount of arousal and stress, and of interpersonal strain and mistrust, prohibits people from focusing on the problem, from open-mindedly generating ideas, and from jointly selecting and implementing adequate problem solutions. Walton (1969) has already provided some qualitative support for the curvilinear relationship between conflict and performance. Using quantitative methodologies, Jehn (1995) found support for such a curvilinear relationship between conflict and individual effectiveness as rated by supervisors. De Dreu (in press) observed such a curvilinear relationship between conflict in work teams, and work-team innovations in two different studies involving a heterogeneous sample of teams from a variety of organizations. Thus, albeit fairly small, the evidence for the information-processing perspective is quite promising.

The *conflict typology framework* relies on the distinction between task conflict and relationship conflict. In essence, it argues that relationship conflict interferes with performing tasks, and thus lowers effectiveness and innovativeness. Task conflict, however, is thought to trigger information processing and to lead participants to consider multiple perspectives and various problem solutions. Task conflict prevents moving to premature consensus, and thus should enhance decision-making quality, individual creativity, and work-team effectiveness in general.

The hypothesis that relationship conflict reduces effectiveness of performance has received ample support (see, e.g., De Dreu & Weingart, 2003b; Jehn, 1995, 1997; Murnighan & Conlon, 1991). However, a recent meta-analysis of the conflict-performance literature provided little support for the hypothesis that task-conflict enhances performance (De Dreu & Weingart, 2003b). This has spurred an interest in developing so-called contingency models, in which task conflict and relationship conflict have different effects on work-team effectiveness depending on specific circumstances, including team tasks, team climate, conflict norms, and conflict management strategies (De Dreu & Weingart, 2003a; Jehn & Bendersky, 2003; see also Simons & Peterson, 2000; Tjosvold, 1998).

EXPANDING THE FIELD: SATISFACTION, WELL-BEING, AND OCCUPATIONAL HEALTH

Much of the work on conflict has, as mentioned, adapted a rather myopic perspective and focused on relatively short-term consequences for individual and work-team effectiveness. To take an example from nearby, consider the study by De Dreu and Van Vianen (2001). In that study relationship conflict in work teams was measured along with the ways these teams managed their relationship conflicts and their work-team effectiveness. The results from this cross-sectional study reveal that dealing with relationship conflict through collaborating and contending is related to much poorer effectiveness than avoiding as a way to manage relationship conflict at all. The authors concluded that avoiding and inaction in relationship conflict and a "let's agree to disagree" strategy may be much more effective than researchers and practitioners tend to assume.

Whereas the conclusions reached by De Dreu and Van Vianen (2001) may be valid and useful, it should be emphasized that their cross-sectional study spanned a time period of only 6 months (the time frame participants had to adopt when answering questions). The study was not prospective in nature, and we cannot know whether avoiding and inaction in the face of relationship conflict might, in fact, have relatively positive effects on team effectiveness in the short run, but highly detrimental consequences in the long run. The detrimental consequences may be in terms of team effectiveness, but they may also be in terms of reduced job satisfaction, lowered identification with the team, reduced commitment to contribute, and ill-health. Ample research in organizational psychology, as well as common sense, tells us that such outcomes easily offset the positive effects one may witness in the short run.

The above example is a rule rather than an exception in the domain of conflict and negotiation research. As mentioned, this and the following articles consider both theoretically and empirically what other consequences conflict at work can have, besides its well-documented effects on individual and work-team effectiveness. We first take a look at satisfaction. We then move on and review recent work on conflict and individual health and well-being.

JOB SATISFACTION

In a recent meta-analysis, De Dreu and Weingart (2003a) summarized 15 studies of work teams in which conflict as well as job satisfaction was measured. Their results showed a strong and negative correlation between relationship conflict and satisfaction, and a moderate and negative correlation between task conflict and satisfaction. From this meta-analysis it thus follows that there are relations between conflict and satisfaction. What we do not know is how these relations come about—does conflict impact job satisfaction, or does job satisfaction lead to conflict? Perhaps there is a recursive cycle, with satisfaction influencing conflict and conflict subsequently influencing job satisfaction. Finally, it may well be that there are third variables involved. Perhaps conflict and job satisfaction are to some degree the product of one and the same stable individual difference.

Locke (1976) defined job satisfaction as a pleasurable or positive emotional state resulting from the appraisal of one's job or job experiences. Judge and Hulin (1993) have identified three different approaches to job satisfaction. The first views job satisfaction as resulting from *stable individual differences* that could even have their roots in the individual's genetic inheritance (e.g., Griffin & Bateman, 1986). The second approach sees job satisfaction as the result of *social information processing*—job satisfaction is construed and developed out of experiences and information provided by others at work (e.g., Salancik & Pfeffer, 1977). The third approach is a *job-as-information perspective*. It argues that a person's job satisfaction is influenced directly by the characteristics of his or her job, and the extent to which those characteristics match what that person wants in a job (e.g., Hackman & Oldham, 1976).

The three perspectives on job satisfaction each suggest a different prediction with regard to the causal relationship between conflict and job satisfaction. The individual differences perspective suggests the possibility that some people more easily feel happy in their jobs, and less easily get into conflict and disputes with others. Take as an example individual differences in positive versus negative affectivity. Whereas some people have high chronic levels of positive affectivity, others have relatively high chronic levels of negative affectivity. Whereas the former feel calm, happy, patient, and optimistic, the latter tend to feel down, depressed, sad, nervous, and unhappy. An important hypothesis to test is that those with high levels of chronic positive affectivity are (a) less likely to get into conflicts with others and, if they do, to manage these in rather constructive ways, and entirely independently, and (b) more likely to feel happy about their jobs, and life in general.

The social information-processing perspective on job satisfaction suggests conflict may directly influence job satisfaction (e.g., Salancik & Pfeffer, 1977). Interestingly, it is not so much the focal individual's conflicts that matter, but instead the conflicts he or she witnesses in the workplace. Employees working in groups or departments with relatively high levels of conflict around them may come to conclude that there is a lot wrong with the department, the people in it, and the jobs they are performing. This in turn lowers their positive feelings about their own job.

The job-as-information perspective, finally, suggests that job satisfaction acts as a precursor to conflict in the work place. Within this framework, it is the features of the job itself that produce more or less satisfaction with that job. Low job satisfaction thus is a result of the job, and not so much of conflicts at work. However, as we will see in the next section, low job satisfaction, and low levels of well-being in general, may very well trigger task as well as relationship conflicts between oneself and one's colleagues or supervisor.

WELL-BEING AND OCCUPATIONAL HEALTH

For a variety of reasons that are unrelated to conflict at work, employees may experience reduced well-being and feel less committed to their work. We know that psychosomatic complaints and stress negatively affect an individual's problem-solving capacity and his or her task focus. Enduring stress further increases irritability, and tendencies to distance oneself from one's (social) environment. Put differently, employees under stress, and those with poor health and low well-being, may trigger conflicts with colleagues and are more prone to get into conflict with their colleagues and supervisors due to poor performance.

Well-being is also influenced by conflict. Conflict-related emotions such as anger, disgust, and fear may affect one's self-esteem and require cognitive resources to cope with the situation. In the long run, when conflict persists or even intensifies, the concomitant continuously high levels of stress hormones deplete the physiological system (McEwen, 1998), and result in psychosomatic complaints including enduring headaches and upset stomachs (Pennebaker, 1982). Enduring conflict deteriorates the work climate and may reinforce rumination, alcohol intake, and sleep problems. This, in turn, may negatively affect the physical and psychological well-being of the individuals involved (Cooper & Marshall, 1976; Dana & Griffin, 1999). In other words, the occurrence of conflict at work results in a decline in physical and psychic functioning which, in the long run, produces psychosomatic complaints, and feelings of burnout.

Related to conflict at work is workplace bullying. A recent survey by the European Foundation for the Improvement of Living and Working Conditions revealed that 9% of the 21,500 respondents was confronted with bullying behaviour (Merllié & Paoli, 2001), that 2% faced sexual harassment, and that 2% faced (threats of) physical violence from co-workers or supervisors (e.g., Zapf, Knorz, & Kulla, 1996b). Other surveys indicate that exposure to systematic bullying can result in severe health problems, as exemplified by psychosomatic complaints and posttraumatic anxiety disorders (Einarsen, 1999).

Less severe forms of conflict have a similar, though less severe, impact on health and well-being. Spector and Jex (1998) summarize the findings of 13 samples involving over 3000 employees. Their meta-analysis showed a moderate and positive correlation between conflict at work and psychosomatic complaints. Spector, Chen, and O'Connell (2000) found positive and moderate correlations between conflict at work and anxiety and frustration, and a small but significant correlation between conflict at work and physical complaints. Other studies reported highly similar results (see, e.g., Beehr, Drexler, & Faulkner, 1997; Frone, 2000; Hillhouse, 1997; Rahim, 1983; Shirom & Mayer, 1993). Finally, a number of studies revealed moderately positive correlations between conflict at work and the exhaustion dimension of burnout (Brondolo et al., 1998; Leiter, 1991; Rainey, 1999; Richardsen, Burke, & Leiter, 1992; Taylor, Daniel, Leith, & Burke, 1990; Van Dierendonck, Schaufeli, & Sixma, 1994).

Taken together, there is reason to expect poor health to trigger conflict at work, and to expect that conflict at work deteriorates health, resulting in psychosomatic complaints and feelings of burnout. Empirical research corroborates these ideas, although it must be noted that this research base is largely cross-sectional. Future research is needed that develops longitudinal designs, and that explicitly focuses on moderators of the conflict – well-being relationship. Such moderators might include personality dispositions, conflict management strategies, and organizational characteristics, to name but a few.

THE CURRENT ISSUE: OVERVIEW

In the previous sections we have, with more or less research evidence to build on, speculated about the ways in which job satisfaction, well-being, and occupational health can produce conflict, drive preferences for specific ways of managing conflict, or be the immediate or delayed result of conflict in the workplace. As is evident from our review, research on the interrelations between conflict and other variables than individual and work-team effectiveness is truly in its infancy. Answering the need for more descriptive and explanatory research, the articles in this Special Issue deal with one or more of the issues referred to above in more depth. Each in its own way, and together, they shed light on how conflict theory and research can be connected to contemporary work in organizational psychology on job satisfaction (and related constructs such as commitment and motivation), well-being, and occupational health.

Dijkstra, Van Dierendonck, and Evers report a field study involving a health-care institution. These investigators examined the mediating influence of conflict responses on the relation between conflict and well-being. Using structural equation modelling, support was found for the hypothesis that conflict at work produces the experience of more organizational stress and reduced well-being. Dijkstra and colleagues not only found that conflict positively relates to responses of helplessness and flight behaviour, but also that these responses mediate the effects of conflict on experienced organizational stress.

In a sample of social services workers in the Netherlands, Giebels and Janssen examine whether the intrapsychic tension associated with interpersonal conflict at work, i.e., conflict stress, is responsible for reduced well-being in terms of emotional exhaustion, absenteeism, and turnover intentions. Their results supported this prediction: Conflict stress was positively related to emotional exhaustion, absenteeism, and turnover intentions. Importantly, their study also identified third party help as an additional style of conflict management next to more traditional styles such as collaborating and contending. Interestingly, the negative relationships between conflict stress on the one hand, and emotional exhaustion, absenteeism, and turnover intentions on the other, were strong among employees who report low third-party help and nonexistent for respondents who report high third-party help. Based on these and related findings, Giebels and Janssen therefore conclude that third-party help appears a successful conflict management strategy to prevent negative outcomes of interpersonal conflict in organizations.

Guerra, Martínez, Munduate, and Medina examine the relations between task and relationship conflict on the one hand, and job satisfaction and well-being on the other. Moreover, their work considers the moderating role of organizational culture. These authors studied the relationships between conflict and job satisfaction and well-being both within a public organization with a low goal-oriented culture, and within a private organization with a high goal-oriented culture. The results of their study reveal that within both organizations relationship conflict was negatively related to job satisfaction and well-being. Furthermore, task conflicts were negatively related to job satisfaction and well-being in the private, high goal-orientation organization but not in the public, low goal-orientation culture. In the latter organizational culture, supporting relations appeared to play a much more important role than goal orientation.

The final article in this Special Issue not only steps away from the traditional focus on individual and group effectiveness, but also redirects attention away from within-group conflict towards between-group disputes. Specifically, Richter, Scully, and West criticize that scholars and practitioners alike tend to see the absence of conflict between groups as indicative of effective intergroup relations within organizations. The authors demarcate a different approach and propose alternative criteria of intergroup effectiveness incorporating soft outcomes, e.g., team members' value judgements about unreasonable time and human resources spent in coordination and negotiation with other teams. They assess the psychometric characteristics of a short measure based on these criteria and discuss implications for both the study of intergroup relations and conflict theory.

The collection of articles in the Special Issue expands conflict theory in a number of ways. Besides the specific conclusions that derive from each of the articles separately, we also see emerging support for the general contention that the traditional focus on conflict, conflict management, and individual and work-team effectiveness incorrectly and unnecessarily narrows the width and breadth of conflict theory. We hope the articles in this Special Issue serve as a first solid step towards a theory of conflict at work that is not only internally consistent and empirically supported, but also well-connected to other relevant processes and phenomena in organizational psychology and organizational behaviour.

REFERENCES

Amason, A. C. (1996). Distinguishing the effects of functional and dysfunctional conflict on strategic decision making: Resolving a paradox for top management groups. *Academy of Management Journal, 39,* 123–148.

Beehr, T. A., Drexler, J. A., & Faulkner, S. (1997). Working in small family businesses: Empirical comparisons to non-family businesses. *Journal of Organizational Behavior, 18,* 297–312.

Blake, R., & Mouton, J. S. (1964). *The managerial grid.* Houston, TX: Gulf Publishing Co.

Broadbent, D. E. (1972). *Decision and stress.* New York: Academic Press.

Brondolo, E., Masha, R., Stores, J., Stockhammer, T., Tunick, W., Melhado, E., & Karlin, W. A. (1998). *Journal of Applied Social Psychology, 28,* 2089–2118.

Carnevale, P. J. D., & Pruitt, D. G. (1992). Negotiation and mediation. *Annual Review of Psychology, 43,* 531–582.

Cooper, C. L., & Marshall, J. (1976). Occupational sources of stress: A review of the literature relating to coronary heart disease and mental ill health. *Journal of Occupational Psychology, 49,* 11–28.

Dana, K., & Griffin, R. W. (1999). Health and well-being in the workplace: A review and synthesis of the literature. *Journal of Management, 25,* 357–384.

De Dreu, C. K. W. (in press). When too much and too little hurts: Evidence for a curvilinear relationship between task conflict and innovation in teams. *Journal of Management.*

De Dreu, C. K. W., & Carnevale, P. J. D. (2003). Motivational bases for information processing and strategic choice in conflict and negotiation. In M. P. Zanna (Ed.), *Advances in experimental social psychology* (Vol. 35, pp. 235–291). New York: Academic Press.

De Dreu, C. K. W., Harinck, F., & Van Vianen, A. E. M. (1999). Conflict and performance in groups and organizations. In C. L. Cooper & I. T. Robertson (Eds.), *International review of industrial and organizational psychology* (Vol. 14, pp. 376–405). Chichester, UK: Wiley.

De Dreu, C. K. W., & Van de Vliert, E. (Eds.). (1997). *Using conflict in organizations.* London: Sage.

De Dreu, C. K. W., & Van Vianen, A. E. M. (2001). Responses to relationship conflict and team effectiveness. *Journal of Organizational Behavior, 22,* 309–328.

De Dreu, C. K. W., & Weingart, L. R. (2003a). Task versus relationship conflict, team member satisfaction, and team effectiveness: A meta-analysis. *Journal of Applied Psychology, 88,* 741–749.

De Dreu, C. K. W., & Weingart, L. R. (2003b). Toward a contingency theory of conflict and performance in groups and organizational teams. In M. A. West, D. Tjosvold, & K. Smith (Eds.), *International handbook of organizational teamwork and cooperative working* (pp. 151–166). Chichester, UK: Wiley.

De Dreu, C. K. W., Weingart, L. R., & Kwon, S. (2000). Influence of social motives in integrative negotiation: A meta-analytic review and test of two theories. *Journal of Personality and Social Psychology, 78,* 889–905.

Diener, E. (1984). Subjective well-being. *Psychological Bulletin, 95,* 542–575.

Dijkstra, M. T. M., Evers, A., Van Dierendonck, D., & De Dreu, C. K. W. (2003, June 11–14). *Conflict, conflict management, and well-being: The moderating influence of personality.* Paper presented at the 11th congress of the European Association for Work and Organizational Psychology, Lisbon, Portugal.

Dijkstra, M. T. M., Van Dierendonck, D., & Evers, A. (this issue). Responding to conflict at work and individual well-being: The mediating role of flight behaviour and feelings of helplessness. *European Journal of Work and Organizational Psychology, 14,* 119–135.

Einarsen, S. (1999). The nature and causes of bullying at work. *International Journal of Manpower, 20,* 16–27.

Friedman, R. A., Tidd, S. T., Currall, S. C., & Tsai, J. C. (2000). What goes around comes around: The impact of personal conflict style on work group conflict and stress. *International Journal of Conflict Management, 10,* 17–35.

Frone, M. R. (2000). Interpersonal conflict at work and psychological outcomes: Testing a model among young workers. *Journal of Occupational Health Psychology, 5,* 246–255.

Giebels, E., & Janssen, O. (this issue). Conflict stress and reduced well-being at work: The buffering effect of third-party help. *European Journal of Work and Organizational Psychology, 14,* 137–155.

Griffin, R. W., & Bateman, T. S. (1986). Job satisfaction and organizational commitment. In C. Cooper & I. T. Robertson (Eds.), *International review of industrial and organizational psychology* (Vol. 8, pp. 157–188). Chichester, UK: Wiley.

Guerra, J. M., Martínez, I., Munduate, L., & Medina, F. J. (this issue). A contingency perspective on the study of the consequences of conflict types: The role of organizational culture. *European Journal of Work and Organizational Psychology, 14,* 157–176.

Hackman, J. R., & Oldham, G. R. (1976). Motivation through the design of work: Test of a theory. *Organizational Behavior and Human Performance, 16,* 250–279.

Hillhouse, J. J. (1997). Investigating stress effect patterns in hospital staff nurses: Results of a cluster analysis. *Social Science and Medicine, 45*, 1781–1788.

Jehn, K. (1995). A multimethod examination of the benefits and detriments of intragroup conflict. *Administrative Science Quarterly, 40*, 256–282.

Jehn, K. A. (1997). A qualitative analysis of conflict types and dimensions in organizational groups. *Administrative Science Quarterly, 42*, 530–557.

Jehn, K., & Bendersky, C. (2003). Intragroup conflict in organizations: A contingency perspective on the conflict–outcome relationship. In R. M. Kramer & B. M. Staw (Eds.), *Research in organizational behavior* (Vol. 25, pp. 187–242.) New York: Elsevier JAI.

Judge, T. A., & Hulin, C. L. (1993). Job satisfaction as a reflection of disposition: A multiple source causal analysis. *Organizational Behavior and Human Decision Processes, 56*, 388–421.

Leiter, M. P. (1991). Coping patterns as predictors of burnout: The function of control and escapists coping patterns. *Journal of Organizational Behavior, 12*, 123–144.

Locke, E. A. (1976). The nature and causes of job satisfaction. In M. Dunnette (Ed.), *Handbook of industrial and organizational psychology* (pp. 323–349). Chicago: Rand McNally.

McEwen, B. S. (1998). Protective and damaging effects of stress mediators. *Seminars in Medicine of the Beth Israel Deaconess Medical Center, 338*, 171–179.

Merllié, D., & Paoli, P. (2001). *Ten years of working conditions in the European Union.* Dublin, Ireland: European Foundation for the Improvement of Living and Working Conditions.

Murnighan, J. K., & Conlon, D. E. (1991). The dynamics of intense work groups: A study of British string quartets. *Administrative Science Quarterly, 36*, 165–186.

Pennebaker, J. W. (1982). *The psychology of physical symptoms.* New York: Springer Verlag.

Pruitt, D. G. (1998). Social conflict. In D. Gilbert, S. T. Fiske, & G. Lindzey (Eds.), *Handbook of social psychology* (4th ed., Vol. 2, pp. 89–150). New York: McGraw-Hill.

Pruitt, D. G., & Rubin, J. (1986). *Social conflict: Escalation, stalemate and settlement.* New York: Random House.

Rahim, A. (1983). Measurement of organizational conflict. *Journal of General Psychology, 109*, 188–199.

Rainey, D. W. (1999). Stress, burnout and intention to terminate among umpires. *Journal of Sport Behavior, 18*, 312–323.

Richardsen, A. M., Burke, R. J., & Leiter, M. P. (1992). Occupational demands, psychological burnout and anxiety among hospital personnel in Norway. *Anxiety, Stress, and Coping, 5*, 55–68.

Richter, A., Scully, J., & West, M. (this issue). Intergroup conflict and intergroup effectiveness in organizations: Theory and scale development. *European Journal of Work and Organizational Psychology, 14*, 177–203.

Robinson, S. L., & Bennett, R. J. (1995). A typology of deviant workplace behaviors: A multidimensional scaling study. *Academy of Management Journal, 38*, 555–572.

Salancik, G. R., & Pfeffer, J. (1977). An examination of need satisfaction models of job satisfaction. *Administrative Science Quarterly, 22*, 427–456.

Shirom, A., & Mayer, A. (1993). Stress and strain among union lay officials and rank-and-file members. *Journal of Organizational Behavior, 14*, 401–413.

Simons, T. L., & Peterson, R. S. (2000). Task conflict and relationship conflict in top management teams: The pivotal role of intragroup trust. *Journal of Applied Psychology, 85*, 102–111.

Spector, P. E., Chen, P. Y., & O'Connell, B. J. (2000). A longitudinal study of relations between job stressors and job strains while controlling for prior negative affectivity and strains. *Journal of Applied Psychology, 85*, 211–218.

Spector, P. E., & Jex, S. M. (1998). Development of four self-report measures of job stressors and strain: Interpersonal Conflict at Work Scale, Organizational Constraints Scale, Quantitative Workload Inventory, and Physical Symptoms Inventory. *Journal of Occupational Health Psychology, 3,* 356–367.

Taylor, A., Daniel, J. V., Leith, L., & Burke, R. J. (1990). Perceived stress, psychological burnout and paths to turnover intentions among sport officials. *Applied Sport Psychology, 2,* 84–97.

Thomas, K. W. (1992). Conflict and negotiation processes in organizations. In M. D. Dunnette & L. M. Hough (Eds.), *Handbook of industrial and organizational psychology* (2nd ed., pp. 651–717). Palo Alto, CA: Consulting Psychologists Press.

Tjosvold, D. (1998). Cooperative and competitive goal approach to conflict: Accomplishments and challenges. *Applied Psychology: An International Review, 47,* 285–342.

Van de Vliert, E. (1997). *Complex interpersonal conflict behaviour.* Hove, UK: Psychology Press.

Van Dierendonck, D., Schaufeli, W. B., & Sixma, H. (1994). Burnout among general practitioners: A perspective from equity theory. *Journal of Social and Clinical Psychology, 13,* 86–100.

Wall, J., & Callister, R. (1995). Conflict and its management. *Journal of Management, 21,* 515–558.

Walton, R. E. (1969). *Interpersonal peacemaking: Confrontations and third party consultation.* Reading, MA: Addison-Wesley.

Yerkes, R. M., & Dodson, J. D. (1908). The relation of strength of stimulus to rapidity of habit formation. *Journal of Comparative Neurological Psychology, 18,* 459–482.

Zapf, D., Knorz, C., & Kulla, M. (1996b). On the relationship between mobbing factors and job content, social work environment, and health outcomes. *European Journal of Work and Organizational Psychology, 5,* 215–237.

EUROPEAN JOURNAL OF WORK AND
ORGANIZATIONAL PSYCHOLOGY
2005, 14 (2), 119–135

Responding to conflict at work and individual well-being: The mediating role of flight behaviour and feelings of helplessness

Maria T. M. Dijkstra, Dirk van Dierendonck, and Arne Evers

University of Amsterdam, The Netherlands

A field study involving a healthcare institution was conducted, to examine the mediating influence of conflict responses on the relation between conflict and well-being. We tested the hypothesis that conflict at work and its responses resulted in the experience of more organizational stress and therefore in reduced well-being. Using structural equation modelling we found support for our hypotheses. We not only showed that conflict was positively related to helplessness and flight behaviour, but also that these responses mediated between conflict and organizational stress. Finally, increases in experienced organizational stress reduced well-being. Implications for conflict theory and well-being in organizations are discussed.

Conflict is strongly associated with working in organizations and in the near future this relationship probably will become even stronger. With organizations becoming increasingly delayered in their structure (Pfeffer, 1998), and with the growing diversity of the work force (Williams & O'Reilly, 1998) as well as the higher level of education and specialization of the employees, the need to coordinate and work together is increasing. The consequential heterogeneous value and belief systems combined with the growing information dependency bears the potential for misunderstanding, disagreement, and irritation (De Dreu, Van Dierendonck, & De Best-Waldhober, 2002).

What consequences conflict has largely depends on the way employees respond to the conflict situation. Although there are some positive outcomes that can be the result of coping constructively with conflict (Arnold & O'Connor, 1999; De Dreu, Weingart, & Kwon, 2000), hostile exchanges and competitive approaches often produce increased absenteeism, turnover, and

Correspondence should be addressed to Maria Dijkstra, Department of Psychology, University of Amsterdam, Roetersstraat 15, 1018 WB Amsterdam, The Netherlands. Email: M.T.M.Dijkstra@uva.nl

http://www.tandf.co.uk/journals/pp/1359432X.html   DOI: 10.1080/13594320444000254

job dissatisfaction (Spector & Jex, 1998; Tjosvold, 1998). Also, in looking at the consequences of conflict for individual well-being there is a series of studies that show mild to moderate positive correlations between some measure of conflict and psychosomatic complaints, psychological strain, and burnout (e.g., Brondolo et al., 1998; Spector, Chen, & O'Connell, 2000; Van Dierendonck, Schaufeli, & Sixma, 1994).

One conclusion that may be drawn from these studies is that conflict may act as a stressor. However, these studies do not inform us about the nature of the relationship between conflict—the stressor—and the way it is responded to on the one hand and indicators of well-being on the other. The question of *how* conflict is related to deteriorated well-being remains therefore unanswered. Second, until now, the possible mediating intrapersonal processes in the relationship between conflict and individual well-being have been largely ignored. Researchers tend to focus on specific ways of handling conflict and tend to ignore within-person processes. Conflict management is what people who experience conflict intend to do as well as what they actually do (Van de Vliert, 1997). Reacting to a conflict behaviourally though, is not the only way of responding to conflict. In our study we will take a broader perspective and focus on the role of coping mechanisms as ways of responding to conflict, other than conflict management strategies. In trying to shed more light on the nature of the relationship between conflict and individual well-being, we will look upon conflict as a stressor and borrow from approaches used in studying stress.

CONFLICT AS A STRESSOR AND INDIVIDUAL WELL-BEING

Stress research is concerned with the (inadequate) adaptation of individuals to their environment and with the resulting physiological, behavioural, and psychological consequences (Quick, Quick, Nelson, & Hurrell, 1997). As suggested by Hobfoll (1989), loss or the threat of loss is a central element in this process. His theory of conservation of resources is based on the supposition that people try to protect everything, material and immaterial, that they value. These "values" are called resources. An actual or a perceived (imminent) loss of those resources is envisaged as sufficient for producing a reaction of striving to minimize the net loss of resources. This reaction is associated with physiological and psychological responses.

Most research on stress in organizations is concerned with circumstances and events that threaten resources such as the amount of time one has available for task completion, the budgets one can work with, the self-image, or the amount of control one experiences. All of these actual or perceived (job) stressors, may bring about the reaction of striving to minimize the net loss of resources through (mal)adaptive physiological and psychological responses.

In reviewing the literature, Jex and Beehr (1991) specified interpersonal stressors as one of the more detrimental job stressors. As an example, they took the work of Newton and Keenan (1985) who asked young engineers to describe stressful incidents on the job as well as their reactions to these incidents. Interestingly, the most common stressors mentioned were "time-wasters" and interpersonal conflict. Parkes (1986) used a similar strategy to classify stressful incidents among female nursing students and found the most important stressors to be insecurity about knowledge and skills and, again, interpersonal conflict. Smith and Sulsky (1995) surveyed over 600 people in a variety of occupations from three different organizations and found that almost 25% of the respondents nominated interpersonal issues as their most bothersome job stressor (see also Prosser, Johnson, Kuipers, Szmukler, Bebbington, & Thornicroft, 1997). In their examination of daily stressors Bolger, DeLongis, Kessler, and Schilling (1989) found that interpersonal conflicts are by far the most upsetting of all daily stressors, accounting for more than 80% of the explained variance in daily mood. Their results also revealed that conflicts with friends, neighbours, and co-workers are more distressing than those with family members. From the above we may conclude that, indeed, conflict acts a major stressor.

Stressors in general, and conflict in particular, potentially have a strong effect on the well-being of individuals (House, Landis, & Umberson, 1988). Well-being is a subjective experience and can be defined as a person's cognitive and affective evaluations of his or her life (Diener, Lucas, & Oishi, 2002), and as such it refers to the extent that a person feels healthy, satisfied with, and even happy about life (Rainey, 1995; Richardsen, Burke, & Leiter, 1992; Van Dierendonck et al., 1994).

Conflict emerges when an individual or group perceives an interdependent other individual or group to oppose one's own interests, beliefs, values, or perceptions of reality (e.g., De Dreu, Harinck, & Van Vianen, 1999; Pondy, 1992; Pruitt, 1998; Thomas, 1992; Wall & Callister, 1995). The mere experience of discord, divergence of interests, perceptions, values, and beliefs is emotional and likely to elicit anger, disgust, and fear, to threaten one's self-esteem (e.g., Frone, 2000), and to require cognitive resources to cope with the situation. It follows that being in conflict with someone at work brings about strong feelings of unpleasantness and all kinds of other stress responses (e.g., McEwen, 1998; Quick et al., 1997). Indeed in a growing series of studies mild to moderate positive correlations were found between some measure of conflict and psychosomatic complaints, psychological strain, and burnout (for a review, see De Dreu, Van Dierendonck, & Dijkstra, in press) revealing that conflict at work as a stressor might have a significant impact on the well-being of employees. In our study we expect to replicate the negative correlation between the occurrence of conflict and individual well-being (Hypothesis 1).

CONTROL

As stated earlier in this article, the consequences of conflict for individual well-being are dependent on the ways an individual responds to this stressor. Within this context, control is an important psychological construct that in past research has shown its relevance for physical and psychological well-being (e.g., Affleck, Tennen, Pfeiffer, & Fifield, 1987; Skinner, 1996; Steptoe & Appels, 1989). Although individuals differ in the extent to which they like to exercise control over their environment, the need to control the environment seems central to the human species (Burger & Cooper, 1979; Parkes, 1989). The need to master could even be more pervasive than sex, hunger, and thirst in the lives of animal and man and therefore may be one of the strongest motivations and may be a basic human need (e.g., Bandura, 1977; Deci & Ryan, 1985). The advantages of being in control for health and mood have been demonstrated across the human life span, from childhood, through middle adulthood to older adulthood (Abeles, 1990; Averill, 1973; Rodin, 1990; Rothbaum & Weisz, 1989; Shapiro, Sandman, Grossman, & Grossman, 1995). Furthermore, in the area of work and organizational psychology, evidence has been found to suggest that a high level of work control positively influences well-being (Karasek, Theorell, Schwarz, Schnall, Pieper, & Michele, 1988; Perrewe & Ganster, 1989). Consequently, and in accordance with Hobfoll (1989), lack of this important resource or even the threat of losing it is generally believed to induce feelings of distress. In the end, when the situation is perceived as uncontrollable, this actual or perceived loss of resources may result in physical or psychological withdrawal (Seligman, 1979).

A reaction that is likely to occur when an individual faces the threat of losing control symbolized by the stressor is the manifestation of feelings of helplessness. Lack of control initially will lead to feelings of anger and hostility as well as to attempts to regain control. When unsuccessful, the individual will learn that his actions are not connected with the outcome and therefore expect future outcomes also to be independent of his actions. Ultimately the individual gives up any attempt to alter his situation and will consciously experience feelings of helplessness, which up to that point only had been latently present (Seligman, 1979). In the context of conflict at work and following this line of reasoning, it is hypothesized that individuals who experience conflict would develop growing feelings of losing control and, as a result would respond with feelings of helplessness (Hypothesis 2).

Alternatively, however some individuals may prevent feelings of losing control from becoming manifest by mentally withdrawing from situations that cannot be controlled. These individuals will, to put off their minds, engage in all kinds of distracting behaviours (e.g., Carver & Scheier, 1994) trying, in a sense, to flee from the situation. Therefore we expect that the more an individual experiences conflict, the more this individual engages in flight behaviour (Hypothesis 3). In our line of reasoning, evidently one cannot engage in both strategies at the same time, therefore two separate paths appear in our model.

ORGANIZATIONAL STRESS AND WELL-BEING

In responding to stressors in general and to conflict in particular the individual physically (e.g., increased blood pressure), emotionally (e.g., fear), and behaviourally (e.g., withdrawal) responds to the actual, or imminent loss of control. This reactivity is adaptive and in itself not detrimental. Hence one day of extremely hard work, or an incidental large and fundamental conflict with a colleague, will not result in symptoms of deteriorated well-being. However, by experiencing feelings of helplessness, as well as by exhibiting flight behaviour, the actual (conflict) situation will remain unchanged. The problem is not solved. This enduring conflict may deteriorate the work climate and this means that the individual is easily exposed to more and other forms of organizational stress that will force him to adapt to this new perceived or actual threats of losing control. It is this prolonged reactivity, that will disrupt the mental and physical regulation process, and causes symptoms of strain (Gaillard, 1996).

We therefore expect that, through its influence on helplessness and flight behaviour, conflict frequency would be positively related to organizational stress (Hypothesis 4).

Hobfoll (1989) refers to this process as to a "loss-spiral" that exists when initial losses (caused by conflicts) result in a depletion of resources (through their effects on helplessness and flight behaviour), which will over time result in more losses (caused by more organizational stress).

In line with this reasoning, we expect organizational stress to mediate the relationship between helplessness and individual well-being, such that helplessness, through its effect on organizational stress, will result in diminished well-being (Hypothesis 5).

Finally we expect organizational stress to mediate the relationship between flight behaviour and individual well-being such that flight behaviour, through its effect on organizational stress will result in diminished well-being (hypothesis 6). Figure 1 shows our hypothesized model.

METHOD

Sample and procedure

The study participants were members of the nursing and ancillary staff of an institution for people with an acute handicap (e.g., being paralyzed as well as blind). Out of 348 employees, 191 returned the questionnaire (response

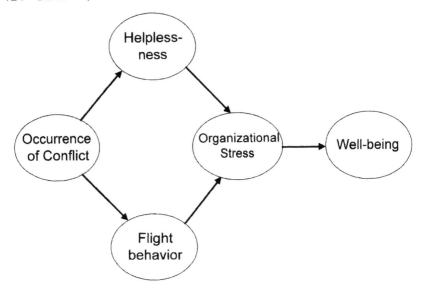

Figure 1. Theoretical model.

rate of 55%) of whom 83% ($N = 159$) were female and 96% ($N = 183$) had the Dutch nationality (4% did not answer this question). The mean age of the employees was 36.5 years ($SD = 9.2$), and average tenure was 5.73 years ($SD = 5.89$). Of all respondents, 20% ($N = 38$) were working 33 hours a week or more, 59% ($N = 112$) were working in irregular shifts and 9% ($N = 17$) fulfilled an executive function.

All employees received a letter from the research team, inviting them to participate in the study emphasizing the importance of participating as well as its voluntary and anonymous character. The letter further explained the purpose of the study as being concerned with work conditions. The executives of 14 subdivisions, which were all part of the institution, but were situated on different locations, distributed the questionnaires. The questionnaires were administered during daytime work hours (they were sent to the home addresses of employees who were not present at that particular point in time).

Measures

Well-being. The Dutch adaptations of the mental and physical health scales (Evers, Frese, & Cooper, 2000) of the Occupational Stress Indicator (OSI) were used to operationalize the well-being of respondents. The mental-health scale consisted of 13 items, tapping a range of mental-health symptoms, which were rated on 6-point Likert-type scales, some of which were reverse scored. A sample item is: "Do you find yourself experiencing fairly long periods in which you feel melancholy for no apparent reason?" The physical-health scale consisted of 13 items relating to somatic symptoms. Respondents were asked to rate the extent to which they experienced the symptoms during the previous 3 months on 6-point Likert-type scales from 1 ("never") to 6 ("frequently"). Sample items are: "Inability to get to sleep", and "Feeling unaccountably tired". For both scales, a lower score indicated greater well-being. The health scale consisted of the items of the combined mental and physical subscales. Cronbach's alphas were .85 and .81, respectively.

Organizational stress.   Three relevant subscales of the Dutch adaptation of the sources-of-stress scale of the OSI (Evers et al., 2000) were used. Each subscale consisted of eight items and measured respectively factors intrinsic to the job (sample item: "Working a lot of hours"); the managerial role (sample item: "Ambiguity about your responsibilities"); and organizational structure and climate (sample item: "Covert discrimination and favouritism"). Respondents were asked to rate the items in terms of the (perceived) degree of pressure each factor may place on them. A 6-point Likert scale was used, ranging from 1 ("a very small degree") to 6 ("a very large degree"). Cronbach's alphas were .80, .86, and .84, respectively.

Flight behaviour.   A subscale of the Dutch adaptation of the Occupational Stress Indicator (Evers et al., 2000) was used to assess this coping strategy. The items were rated on a 6-point Likert scale ranging from 1 ("never") to 6 ("frequently"). Sample items are: "I notice that I drink more alcohol when I have problems", and "When there are problems I tend to watch more TV". Cronbach's alpha was .55.

Helplessness.   We used the Dutch adaptation of the individual influence subscale of the Locus of Control Scale of the OSI (Evers et al., 2000) to measure the respondent's perceptions about the amount of influence any individual can have within the organization. The five items of this scale were rated on a 6-point Likert scale ranging from 1 ("never") to 6 ("frequently"). Sample items are: "I have no say in the assignments I get at my work", and: " My work is just a cog in the machine over which I have little control". Cronbach's alpha was .71.

Occurrence of conflict.   We asked employees how often they experienced conflicts about tasks and personal matters work (two items). The answering scale ranged from 1 ("almost never"), to 5 ("very often"). Cronbach's alpha was .57.

Analysis

Structural equation modelling using Lisrel 8.54 (Jöreskog & Sörbom, 1993) was employed to assess the fit of the proposed model. We performed the two-step structural equation modelling approach recommended by Anderson and Gerbing (1988). First the measurement model was assessed to validate the operationalization of the theoretical constructs. Second, the structural equation model, specifying the relations among the latent variables, was tested. The structural model consists of five hypothetical constructs, or latent variables, that are estimated by one or more empirical, manifest variables that are directly observed. In the measurement model, each latent variable was indicated by either the separate items (i.e., helplessness and flight behaviour) or by the subscales (i.e., physical and mental health). Conflict was estimated by the two items on task and personal conflict as described in the method section.

The goodness-of-fit of the models was evaluated using relative and absolute indices as recommended by Hu and Bentler (1998). The absolute goodness-of-fit indices calculated were the chi-square goodness-of-fit index and the standardized root-mean-square residual (SRMR). A value of .08 or less is considered as indicating a relatively good fit for the SRMR. The relative goodness-of-fit indices computed were the comparative fit index (CFI) and the non-normed fit index (NNFI or TLI). For both indices, values equal or greater than .95 are considered as indicating a good fit.

RESULTS

Measurement model results

Table 1 contains the descriptive statistics and intercorrelations of variables on which the LISREL analyses were based. Table 2 contains the goodness-of-fit statistics obtained from analysing the measurement model. The comparative fit indices show a nonsatisfactory fit to the data, the CFI was .84, the NNFI was .84 and the SRMR was .07.

In order to find out what caused the relatively low fit, we first checked the significance of the factor loadings of the measurement model. They were all significant. The modification indices of the indicators also showed that the low fit was not due to misspecification of the measurement model but due to ignored variance between measurement errors. Ignoring correlated measurement errors in a model affects not only the goodness-of-fit indices but also the parameters in the model (Reddy, 1992). Allowing those measurement errors to be correlated will result in a more accurate estimation of the structural parameters. The error variances of eight-item pairs were allowed

TABLE 1

Descriptive statistics and intercorrelations of variables (N = 191)

	M	SD	1	2	3	4	5	6	7	8
1. Task conflict	2.37	0.95								
2. Personal conflict	1.85	0.96	.51**							
3. Flight behaviour	1.84	0.51	.21**	.26**	(.55)					
4. Helplessness	4.68	0.76	.18*	.19*	.09	(.71)				
5. Intrinsic work stressors	2.98	1.02	.22**	.18*	.40**	.23**	(.80)			
6. Structure and climate stressors	3.45	1.16	.35**	.31**	.35**	.40**	.65**	(.84)		
7. Role stressors	2.92	1.11	.23**	.21**	.43**	.35**	.82**	.74**	(.86)	
8. Physical health	4.92	0.64	−.18*	−.18*	−.36**	−.19*	−.29**	−.34**	−.34**	(.81)
9. Mental health	3.78	0.40	−.06	−.08	−.33**	.06	−.23**	−.15	−.25**	.42**	(.85)

*p < .05, **p < .01.

TABLE 2
Goodness-of-fit indices for measurement and structural models

	χ^2	df	CFI	NNFI	SRMR
Measurement model	229.30	125	.84	.84	.07
Measurement model, adjusted	154.11	117	.96	.95	.06
Hypothesized model	155.00	122	.96	.96	.06

to correlate. The resulting model provided an excellent fit to the data, the CFI was .96, the NNFI was .95, and the SRMR was .06.

Structural model results

The second phase was the structural modelling procedure. The hypothesized model was fitted to the data. According to both incremental fit indices, the fit of the hypothetical model is quite satisfactory with values of .96 and .96 (see Table 2). This is confirmed by the SRMR that is with a value of .06 below the .08 threshold. We can conclude that this model provided a good fit to the data according to the criteria formulated by Hu and Bentler (1998).

The completely standardized solution of the model (see Figure 2) shows that conflict is positively related to helplessness and flight behaviour. Both helplessness and flight behaviour are related to more organizational stress, which is negatively related to well-being.

Our hypothesized model specified a mediating role of helplessness and flight behaviour between conflict and organizational stress. For a variable to function as a mediator three conditions should be met (Baron & Kenny, 1986): (1) The independent variable should be related to the mediator, (2) the mediator should be related to the outcome variable, and (3) the relation between the independent variable and the outcome variable should be significantly reduced if the paths defined under a and b are controlled for. The correlations in Table 1 showed that originally conflicts, flight behaviour, helplessness and all three of the organization stressors were significantly related, thus satisfying the required conditions for testing mediation. In the final model (Figure 2), there is no direct path between the occurrence of conflict and organizational stress, so condition c holds, flight behaviour and helplessness function as mediators.

DISCUSSION

From past research we know that conflict at work is associated with psychosomatic complaints, and other stress-related indicators such as chronic fatigue (e.g., De Dreu et al., 2002; Spector & Jex, 1998). It was

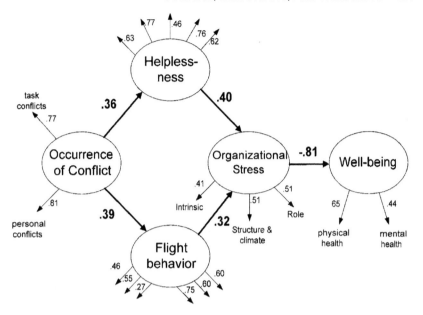

Figure 2. Final model completely standardized solution. The relations between the error terms are not depicted for reasons of clarity.

unclear how responding to this stressor influenced the relationship between the occurrence of conflict and individual well-being. Until now researchers did not address the mediating role of conflict management strategies in the interplay between conflict and well-being. By not restricting ourselves to this behavioural way of responding to conflict (i.e., handling the conflict) but by taking a broader perspective from stress theory, we addressed this issue.

Results of our study confirmed the important role of conflict as a major stressor at work. Furthermore, and in support of our hypotheses results showed that responding to this stressor with feelings of helplessness and with flight behaviour is associated with the experience of more organizational stress, which results in deteriorated well-being. We could also confirm the two separate paths indicating the independence of the constructs of feelings of helplessness and flight behaviour. These results provide further insight into the complex interplay between conflict at work and individual well-being. By looking at conflict as a stressor, the significance of the concept of control helps us to explain how actual or perceived loss of control will determine the choice for particular ways of responding to conflict. In what follows, we address several contributions to conflict theory, and discuss some practical implications of our results.

Contributions to theory

In the past three decades, a tremendous amount of research has focused on the ways people manage conflict in the work place, and how this affects individual and group performance. This research generally shows that under specific conditions, individuals and groups can benefit from conflict—conflict increases individual creativity (Nemeth, 1986), it stimulates group innovation (De Dreu & West, 2001; Lovelace, Shapiro, & Weingart, 2001; West & Anderson, 1996), and when conflict is managed through constructive problem solving, it generally increases individual and group effectiveness (Tjosvold, 1998). This conflict research has, however, largely ignored the potentially detrimental consequences of conflict for employee well-being, and so a one-sided theory tends to emerge.

Studies in the domain of occupational health have dealt with the possible negative consequences of conflict for individual well-being, and these studies generally show negative but small to moderate correlations between conflict at work, and indicators of well-being including psychosomatic complaints, feelings of burnout, and negative affect (De Dreu et al., 2002; Spector & Jex, 1998). Thus, a first contribution of the current work is that it shows that conflict at work can seriously affect employee well-being, and that much of this effect is related to the way individuals respond to the conflict.

We argued and showed that the occurrence of conflict at work tends to be related to increased tendencies to respond to conflict in passive, nonconfronting ways. These types of coping are at odds with findings from earlier research that positive effects of conflict come about especially when conflict is managed in a constructive problem-solving way (Arnold & O'Connor, 1999; De Dreu et al., 2000). We may now conclude that the occurrence of conflict does not automatically trigger this (constructive) problem-solving behaviour and therefore the possible positive consequences of conflict are unlikely to come about in an easy way.

Identifying reduced well-being as a consequence of conflict suggests an ongoing negative spiral (De Dreu et al., 2000; Rubin, Pruitt, & Kim, 1994; Tjosvold, 1998) in which conflict deteriorates well-being, which in turn reduces the employee's propensity to manage the conflict constructively, which in turn raises the probability of future conflict, and so on. Clearly, longitudinal research testing this negative spiral model is needed.

Implications for practice

The strongest implication for practice is that the occurrence of conflict is related to deteriorated well-being, and that the measurement of occurrence of conflict at work should become an important tool for consultants in diagnosing and advising organizations with high rates of turnover, sick leaves, and absenteeism. Furthermore, our work showed that because conflict produces passive and inadequate coping behaviour it will lead to more organizational stress. It follows, that one should fight this natural propensity, that is avoid passivity, and manage the conflict constructively instead.

From the perspective of occupational health, managers and human resource officials may take responsibility and consider conflict and how conflict is dealt with in a serious way. Within the more general framework of the organizational strategy of stress, management, for example training packages and courses, may be offered. These tools may help employees who are in conflict to refrain from passive responses and prevent negative consequences for individual well-being to arise.

Strengths and limitations

Most research on conflict in the work place has focused on behavioural and material outcomes of conflict such as joint outcomes and performance. By doing so, the consequences of conflict in cognitive and emotional terms have rarely been considered. In our study we showed that it is just the occurrence of these emotional and cognitive responses to conflict that produce more organizational stress and therefore negatively influences well-being.

Although the results of our study supported our theoretical model, several issues require attention. One is the cross-sectional nature of the study limiting causal interpretations. We propose directional relations between the constructs; however, we cannot rule out the alternative model in which reduced well-being leads to organizational stress, which in turn through the influence of responses of helplessness and flight behaviour results in more conflict. So future research using a cross-lagged design with longitudinal data is needed to further strengthen our theoretical model. Secondly, conflict at work was measured with only two items, and the reader may wonder whether this measure assessed conflict at work in a reliable and valid way. However, the items exclusively focused on the occurrence of conflict, eliminating possible confounding with the way conflicts are managed (Dijkstra, Van Dierendonck, Evers, & De Dreu, 2002). That we replicated past results, showing a moderately negative relation between conflict and individual well-being, provides further confidence in the adequacy of our conflict measure. The internal consistency of the scale that measures flight behaviour was somewhat low (.55). However, one might argue that internal consistency is hardly relevant for this scale, since the items do not refer to a particular underlying construct and therefore need not necessarily correlate (see also Spector & Jex, 1998). The negative impact on the validity of our results is reduced since we analysed the relationships between latent variables.

CONCLUSION

Conflict at work acts as a major stressor and responding to this stressor in passive non confronting ways is not only likely to occur, but will also put into operation a negative spiral. The initial increase in the experience of organizational stress, that is the diminished actual or perceived loss of control will, in the end, result in reduced well-being. It is suggested that the deterioration of well-being may weaken the tendency to respond to conflict in a cooperative way (e.g., problem-solving behaviour). This possibility should be further examined for it is just this cooperative way of responding to conflict that has proven to generate the best results in fighting the negative consequences of conflict.

REFERENCES

Abeles, R. P. (1990). Schemas, sense of control, and aging. In J. Rodin, C. Schooler, & K. W. Schaie (Eds.), *Self-directedness: Causes and effects throughout the life course* (pp. 85–94). Hillsdale, NJ: Lawrence Erlbaum Associates, Inc.

Affleck, G., Tennen, H., Pfeiffer, C., & Fifield, J. (1987). Appraisals of control and predictability in adapting to a chronic disease. *Journal of Personality and Social Psychology, 53,* 273–279.

Anderson, J. C., & Gerbing, D. W. (1988). Structural modeling in practice: A review and recommended two-step approach. *Psychological Bulletin, 103,* 411–423.

Arnold, J. A., & O'Connor, K. M. (1999). Ombudspersons or peers? The effect of third-party expertise and recommendations on negotiation. *Journal of Applied Psychology, 84,* 776–785.

Averill, J. R. (1973). Personal control over aversive stimuli and its relationship to stress. *Psychological Bulletin, 80,* 286–303.

Bandura, A. (1977). *Social learning theory.* Englewood Cliffs, NJ: Prentice Hall.

Baron, R. M., & Kenny, D. A. (1986). The moderator–mediator variable distinction in social psychological research: Conceptual, strategic, and statistical considerations. *Journal of Personality and Social Psychology, 51,* 1173–1182.

Bolger, N., DeLongis, A., Kessler, R. C., & Schilling, E. A. (1989). Effects of daily stress on negative mood. *Journal of Personality and Social Psychology, 57,* 808–818.

Brondolo, E., Masheb, R., Stores, J., Stockhammer, T., Tunick, W., Melhado, E., et al. (1998). Anger-related traits and response to interpersonal conflict among New York City traffic agents. *Journal of Applied Social Psychology, 28,* 2089–2118.

Burger, J. M., & Cooper, H. M. (1979). The desirability of control. *Motivation and Emotion, 3,* 381–393.

Carver, C. S., & Scheier, M. F. (1994). Situational coping and coping dispositions in a stressful transaction. *Journal of Personality and Social Psychology, 56,* 267–283.

Deci, E. L., & Ryan, R. M. (1985). *Intrinsic motivation and self-determination in human behaviour.* New York: Plenum Press.

De Dreu, C. K. W., Harinck, F., & Van Vianen, A. E. M. (1999). Conflict and performance in groups and organizations. In C. L. Cooper & I. T. Robertson (Eds.), *International review of industrial and organizational psychology* (Vol. 14, pp. 369–414). Chichester, UK: John Wiley & Sons.

De Dreu, C. K. W., Van Dierendonck, D., & De Best-Waldhober, M. (2002). Conflict at work and individual well-being. In M. J. Schabracq, C. L. Cooper, & J. A. M. Winnubst (Eds.), *The handbook of work and health psychology* (pp. 495–515). New York: John Wiley & Sons.

De Dreu, C. K. W., Van Dierendonck, D., & Dijkstra, M. T. M. (in press). Conflict at work and individual well-being. *International Journal of Conflict Management.*

De Dreu, C. K. W., Weingart, L. R., & Kwon, S. (2000). Influence of social motives on integrative negotiation: A meta-analytic review and test of two theories. *Journal of Personality and Social Psychology, 78*, 889–905.

De Dreu, C. K. W., & West, M. A. (2001). Minority dissent and team innovation: The importance of participation in decision making. *Journal of Applied Psychology, 86*, 1191–1201.

Diener, E., Lucas, R. E., & Oishi, S. (2002). Subjective well-being: The science of happiness and life satisfaction. In C. R. Snyder & S. J. Lopez (Eds.), *Handbook of positive psychology* (pp. 463–473). Oxford, UK: Oxford University Press.

Dijkstra, M. T. M., Van Dierendonck, D., Evers, A., & De Dreu, C. K. W. (2002). *Conflict, conflict management, and well-being: The moderating role of personality.* Paper presented at the 11th congress of the European Association for Work and Organizational Psychology, Lisbon, Portugal.

Evers, A., Frese, M., & Cooper, C. L. (2000). Revisions and further developments of the occupational stress indicator: LISREL results from four Dutch studies. *Journal of Occupational and Organizational Psychology, 73*, 221–240.

Frone, M. R. (2000). Interpersonal conflict at work and psychological outcomes: Testing a model among young workers. *Journal of Occupational Health Psychology, 5*, 246–255.

Gaillard, A. W. K. (1996). *Stress, produktiviteit en gezondheid* [Stress, productivity and health]. Amsterdam: Uitgeverij Nieuwezijds.

Hobfoll, S. E. (1989). Conservation of resources: A new attempt at conceptualizing stress. *American Psychologist, 40*, 513–524.

House, J. S., Landis, K. R., & Umberson, D. (1988). Social relationships and health. *Science, 241*, 540–545.

Hu, L., & Bentler, P. M. (1998). Fit indices in covariance structure modeling: Sensitivity to under parameterized model misspecification. *Psychological Methods, 3*, 424–453.

Jex, M. S., & Beehr, T. A. (1991). Emerging theoretical and methodological issues in the study of work-related stress. *Research in Personnel and Human Resources Management, 9*, 311–365.

Jöreskog, K., & Sörbom, D. (1993). *LISREL 8 user's reference guide.* Chicago: Scientific Software International.

Karasek, R. A., Theorell, T., Schwarz, J. E., Schnall, P. L., Pieper, C. F., & Michele, J. L. (1988). Job characteristics in relation to the prevalence of myocardial infarction in the US Health Examination Survey (HES) and the Health and Nutrition Examination Survey (HANES). *American Journal of Public Health, 78*, 910–918.

Lovelace, K., Shapiro, D. L., & Weingart, L. R. (2001). Maximizing cross-functional new product teams' innovativeness and constraint adherence: A conflict communications perspective. *Academy of Management Journal, 44*, 779–793.

McEwen, B. S. (1998). Seminars in medicine of the Beth Israel Deaconess Medical Center: Protective and damaging effects of stress mediators. *New England Journal of Medicine, 338*, 171–179.

Nemeth, C. J. (1986). Differential contributions of majority and minority influence. *Psychological Review, 93*, 23–32.

Newton, T. J., & Keenan, A. (1985). Coping with work-related stress. *Human Relations, 38*, 107–126.

Parkes, K. R. (1986). Coping in stressful episodes: The role of individual differences, environmental factors, and situational characteristics. *Journal of Personality and Social Psychology, 51*, 1277–1292.

Parkes, K. R. (1989). Personal control in an occupational context. In A. Steptoe & A. Appels (Eds.), *Stress, personal control and health* (pp. 21–47). Chichester, UK: Wiley.

Perrewe, P. L., & Ganster, D. C. (1989). The impact of job demands and behavioral control on experienced job stress. *Journal of Organizational Behavior, 10*, 1–17.

Pfeffer, J. (1998). Understanding organizations: Concepts and controversies. In D. T. Gilbert, S. T. Fiske, & L. Gardner (Eds.), *The handbook of social psychology* (4th ed., Vol. 2, pp. 733–777). New York: McGraw-Hill.

Pondy, L. (1992). Reflections on organizational conflict. *Journal of Organizational Behavior, 13*, 257–261.

Prosser, D., Johnson, S., Kuipers, E., Szmukler, G., Bebbington, P., & Thornicroft, G. (1997). Perceived sources of work stress and satisfaction among hospital and community mental health staff, and their relation to mental health, burnout and job satisfaction. *Journal of Psychosomatic Research, 43*, 51–59.

Pruitt, D. G. (1998). Social conflict. In D. T. Gilbert, S. T. Fiske, & L. Gardner (Eds.), *The handbook of social psychology* (4th ed., Vol. 2, pp. 470–503). New York: McGraw-Hill.

Quick, J. C., Quick, J. D., Nelson, D. L., & Hurrell, J. J., Jr. (1997). *Preventive stress management in organizations*. Washington, DC: American Psychological Association.

Rainey, D. W. (1995). Stress, burnout, and intention to terminate among umpires. *Journal of Sport Behavior, 18*, 312–323.

Reddy, S. K. (1992). Effects of ignoring correlated measurement error in structural equation models. *Educational and Psychological Measurement, 52*, 549–570.

Richardsen, A. M., Burke, R. J., & Leiter, M. P. (1992). Occupational demands, psychological burnout and anxiety among hospital personnel in Norway. *Anxiety, Stress, and Coping, 5*, 55–68.

Rodin, J. (1990). Control by any other name: Definitions, concepts, processes. In J. Rodin, C. Schooler, & K. W. Schaie (Eds.), *Selfdirectedness: Causes and effects throughout the life course* (pp. 1–18). Hillsdale, NJ: Lawrence Erlbaum Associates, Inc.

Rothbaum, F. M., & Weisz, J. R. (1989). *Child pathology and the quest for control*. Newbury Park, CA: Sage.

Rubin, J. Z., Pruitt, D. G., & Kim, S. H. (1994). *Social conflict: Escalation, stalemate and settlement*. New York: McGraw-Hill.

Seligman, M. E. (1979). *Helplessness: On depression, development, and death*. Oxford, UK: W. H. Freeman.

Shapiro, D. H., Sandman, C., Grossman, M., & Grossman, B. (1995). Aging and sense of control. *Psychological Reports, 76*, 1–3.

Skinner, E. A. (1996). A guide to constructs of control. *Journal of Personality and Social Psychology, 71*, 549–570.

Smith, C. S., & Sulsky, L. (1995). An investigation of job-related coping strategies across multiple stressors and samples. In L. R. Murphy, J. J. Hurrell Jr., S. L. Sauter, & G. P. Keita (Eds.), *Job stress interventions* (pp. 109–123). Washington, DC: American Psychological Association.

Spector, P. E., Chen, P. Y., & O'Connell, B. J. (2000). A longitudinal study of relations between job stressors and job strains while controlling for prior negative affectivity and strains. *Journal of Applied Psychology, 85*, 211–218.

Spector, P. E., & Jex, S. M. (1998). Development of four self-report measures of job stressors and strain: Interpersonal Conflict at Work Scale, Organizational Constraints Scale, Quantitative Workload Indicator, and Physical Symptoms Indicator. *Journal of Occupational Health Psychology, 3*, 356–367.

Steptoe, A., & Appels, A. (Eds.). (1989). *Stress, personal control and health*. Chichester, UK: John Wiley & Sons.

Thomas, K. W. (1992). Conflict and negotiation processes in organizations. In M. D. Dunnette & L. M. Hough (Eds.), *Handbook of industrial and organizational psychology* (2nd ed., Vol. 3, pp. 651–717). Palo Alto, CA: Consulting Psychologists Press.

Tjosvold, D. (1998). Cooperative and competitive goal approach to conflict: Accomplishments and challenges. *Applied Psychology: An International Review, 47*, 285–342.

Van de Vliert, E. (1997). *Complex interpersonal conflict behavior.* Hove, UK: Psychology Press.

Van Dierendonck, D., Schaufeli, W. B., & Sixma, H. J. (1994). Burnout among general practitioners: A perspective from equity theory. *Journal of Social and Clinical Psychology, 13*, 86–100.

Wall, J. A., & Callister, R. R. (1995). Conflict and its management. *Journal of Management, 21*, 515–558.

West, M. A., & Anderson, N. R. (1996). Innovation in top management teams. *Journal of Applied Psychology, 81*, 680–693.

Williams, K. Y., & O'Reilly, C. A., III. (1998). Demography and diversity in organizations: A review of 40 years of research. *Research in Organizational Behavior, 20*, 77–140.

EUROPEAN JOURNAL OF WORK AND
ORGANIZATIONAL PSYCHOLOGY
2005, 14 (2), 137–155

Conflict stress and reduced well-being at work: The buffering effect of third-party help

Ellen Giebels and Onne Janssen

University of Groningen, The Netherlands

This study among 108 Dutch social services workers examined whether particularly the intrapsychic tension directly associated with interpersonal conflict at work, i.e., conflict stress, is responsible for reduced well-being in terms of emotional exhaustion, absenteeism, and turnover intentions. Furthermore, we explored whether these detrimental effects were buffered by third-party help. Factor analyses showed that third-party help could be considered an additional conflict management style, next to more traditional behavioural styles such as problem solving and forcing. As expected, conflict stress was positively related to emotional exhaustion, absenteeism, and turnover intentions even when controlled for task and relationship conflict. Furthermore, this relationship was strong for respondents who report low third-party help and nonexistent for respondents who report high third-party help. These findings suggest that third-party help is a successful conflict management strategy to prevent negative outcomes of interpersonal conflict in organizations.

Although conflict at work might be functional under specific circumstances (Amason, 1996; De Dreu & Van de Vliert, 1997; Jehn, 1995), recent research also indicates that interpersonal conflict has detrimental consequences for individual well-being in both the short and the long run (e.g., De Dreu, Van Dierendonck, & De Best-Waldhober, 2002; Frone, 2000; Spector & Jex, 1998). In this article, we argue that particularly the intrapsychic tension directly associated with interpersonal conflict, i.e., conflict stress, is responsible for reduced well-being in terms of emotional exhaustion, absenteeism, and turnover intentions. Furthermore, we propose that these detrimental effects of conflict stress might be buffered by third-party help, a conflict management style that is strongly on the rise in both academia and practice. Below, we first define the concept of conflict stress and discuss how it deteriorates individual well-being. Then, we provide the rationale for the

Correspondence should be addressed to Ellen Giebels, University of Groningen, Grote Kruisstraat 2/1, 9712 TS, Groningen, The Netherlands. Email: e.giebels@ppsw.rug.nl

We would like to thank Alette Zijlstra and Luuk Giebels for their help in collecting the data.

http://www.tandf.co.uk/journals/pp/1359432X.html   DOI: 10.1080/13594320444000236

notion that third-party help can buffer the detrimental effects of conflict stress for individual well-being.

INTERPERSONAL CONFLICT AT WORK

Individuals are in conflict when they are obstructed or irritated by another individual and inevitably react to it in a beneficial or costly way (Van de Vliert, 1997). In a similar vein, De Dreu, Harinck, and Van Vianen (1999) define conflict as the tension an individual experiences because of perceived differences with others. These definitions clearly show that workplace conflict is inextricably bound up with more or less psychic tension or conflict stress. This solidarity between conflict issues and feelings of tension and stress can be explained from occupational stress theory and research (e.g., Jex, 1998). Although interpersonal conflict in the workplace has not been studied extensively in the occupational stress literature, there is growing evidence that this may be one of the most important stressors (Keenan & Newton, 1985; Spector & Jex, 1998). Two complementary processes may explain the close bond between conflict and feelings of arousal, tension, or stress. Firstly, conflict comes hand in hand with feelings of being obstructed in one's goal-directed actions. This obstruction may trigger feelings of reduced control and increased uncertainty, two conditions that have been considered important prerequisites of a stress response (Quick, Quick, Nelson, & Hurrell, 1997; Sutton & Kahn, 1987). Second, conflict threatens one's self-esteem (cf. De Dreu et al., 2002), especially when it concerns conflict with another group member. In general, group membership fulfils a generic need to establish positive and enduring relationships with other people (Baumeister & Leary, 1985). Employees want to be liked by their colleagues because this helps them to maintain a positive social identity (Fiske, 1992). Following this line of reasoning, conflict with co-workers is stressful in itself because it undermines one's sense of self and similarity with others (cf. Frone, 2000).

Conflict may relate to task-oriented or relationship-oriented dissent (Janssen, Van de Vliert, & Veenstra, 1999; Jehn, 1995; Simons & Peterson, 2000). Task conflict refers to disagreements about the work to be done, while relationship conflict refers to identity-oriented issues whereby personal beliefs and values come into play. An important implication of the above line of reasoning is that conflict is inextricably bound up with stress regardless of the type of conflict one experiences. Both task and relationship conflict trigger feelings of reduced control and undermine an individual's sense of self and similarity with others. The latter consequence might be particularly true for relationship conflict, as in this type of conflict identity-oriented issues are at stake. Therefore, we propose the following:

Hypothesis 1: Conflict stress is positively related to the occurrence of conflict; this relationship between stress and conflict is stronger for relationship conflict than task conflict.

CONFLICT AND WELL-BEING AT WORK

As elaborated on above, both task conflict over substantive issues as well as relationship conflict referring to interpersonal dynamics are inextricably bound up with tension, arousal, and stress. However, we expect that individuals experience more stress in response to relationship conflict than task conflict. Differentiating between task conflict and relationship conflict may also be important in light of research suggesting that especially relationship conflict has negative consequences, while task conflict may turn out positively. Research by Jehn (1995) shows, for example, that task conflict stimulates creativity and divergent thinking, especially in nonroutine situations (see also, Janssen et al., 1999; Simons & Peterson, 2000). Accordingly, there is a growing consensus in the literature that while relationship conflict usually hurts team and individual functioning, task conflict can be beneficial (Amason, 1996; De Dreu & Van de Vliert, 1997; Simons & Peterson, 2000; cf. De Dreu & Weingart, 2003).

A recent meta-analytical study by De Dreu and Weingart (2003), however, undermines this assumption and clearly shows that both task and relationship conflict in teams work out negatively. De Dreu and Weingart explained these effects by arguing that the high level of arousal associated with conflict hinders effective information processing (cf. Brown, 1983; Wall & Callister, 1995). Indeed, research suggests that accurate information exchange is key to finding high quality solutions (e.g., De Dreu, Giebels, & Van de Vliert, 1998; Giebels, De Dreu, & Van de Vliert, 2000). However, as high levels of conflict stress hinder individuals to process and exchange information, conflict tends to intensify and parties are likely to engage in destructive conflict spirals. This will further foster feelings of reduced control and lowered self-esteem leading to reduced levels of individual well-being. In the current study we therefore expect a relationship between conflict stress and three mutually connected indicators of individual well-being at work. First and foremost, emotional exhaustion has been identified as one of the main psychological consequences of enduring distress (Quick et al., 1997). Emotional exhaustion refers to feelings of energy depletion and of being overextended by the demands of one's work. It is originally one of the three aspects of Maslach's (1982) burnout model, but in fact represents the core meaning of burnout (cf. Bakker, Schaufeli, Sixma, Bosveld, & Van Dierendonck, 2000; Cropanzano, Rupp, & Byrne, 2003; Heuven & Bakker, 2003; Pines & Aronson, 1988; Wright & Cropanzano,

1998).[1] The accumulation of conflict stress is also expected to promote two withdrawal coping mechanisms: absenteeism and turnover intentions (Hardy, Woods, & Wall, 2003; Lee & Ashforth, 1996; Wright & Cropanzano, 1998). Absenteeism, a behavioural reaction, may be considered a short-term coping strategy associated with nonparticipation (Quick et al., 1997). Turnover intentions refer to an individual's intent to look actively for employment elsewhere, and therefore may be considered a long-term coping strategy. In sum, we predict that:

Hypothesis 2: Conflict stress is positively associated with emotional exhaustion (2A), absenteeism (2B), and turnover intentions (2C).

THIRD-PARTY HELP

Third-party intervention in workplace conflict has received growing attention from theory (e.g., Elangovan, 1995; Kolb, 1986; Sheppard, 1984) and research (e.g., Arnold & O'Connor, 1999; Karambayya & Brett, 1989; Pinkley, Neale, Brittain, & Northcraft, 1995), as well as the practical field of labour relations, community mediation, and international conflict (cf. Kozan & Ilter, 1994). This attention has resulted in the identification and definition of several third-party roles and strategies. That is, third parties may operate on a neutral basis such as ombudspersons (e.g., Arnold & O'Connor, 1999), or may operate primarily from self-interest—so-called partisan third parties (Conlon & Ross, 1993)—such as managers trying to settle a dispute between subordinates (e.g., Pinkley et al., 1995). Generally, a distinction is made between third parties with process control, such as a mediator, and more autocratic third parties with decision control, such as an arbiter. In comparing both types, research clearly shows that interventions through process control render more positive outcomes than interventions through decision control. Process control interventions produce better quality outcomes and more satisfied parties; partly because they are considered more procedurally fair (Karambayya & Brett, 1989; Karambayya, Brett, & Lytle, 1992). As a consequence, conflict parties also prefer mediation over other forms of third-party intervention (Karambayya & Brett, 1989; Karambayya et al., 1992; Lewicki & Sheppard, 1985).

Conflicting employees can take the initiative to ask a third party to help them to derive structure and meaning in the stressful conflict situation (Volkema, Farquhar, & Bergmann, 1996). In line with Ting-Toomey and

---

[1]The other two aspects of the burnout concept, depersonalization and diminished personal accomplishments, have been criticized for being confounded with related concepts such as self-reliance and self-esteem (Shirom, 1989).

Oetzel (2001) we propose that making use of third-party help may be regarded an additional conflict management style, next to more traditional conflict handling styles such as forcing, problem solving, accommodating, and avoiding. Ting-Toomey and Oetzel (2001; see also Ting-Toomey, Yee-Yung, Shapiro, Garcia, Wright, & Oetzel, 2000) provided theoretical and empirical support for this proposition. They defined third-party help in terms of process control as "involving an outsider to mediate the conflict". Defined like this, third-party help may be particularly beneficial in promoting accurate information processing by clarifying the real issues at stake and by setting out procedures to go about the conflict. By applying these interventions, a third party cannot issue binding settlements, but rather help stressful conflict parties to recover their control over the process and outcomes of their disputes and to restore their relationship (Arnold & O'Connor, 1999). Consequently, third-party help may buffer the negative consequences of conflict stress, by helping those employees that experience conflict-related stress to break through negative conflict spirals. As such, the conflict management style of third-party help should be theoretically distinguished from social support, a factor that has been previously identified as a buffer to the negative effects of job stressors (e.g., Cohen & Wills, 1985; Greenglass, Fiksenbaum, & Burke, 1994). While social support reflects the general perception of whether one feels surrounded by others who may offer desirable comfort or advice (Quick et al., 1997), third-party help refers to the specific conflict management style of actively involving a third party in a dispute. All in all, we hypothesize the following:

Hypothesis 3: The relationship between conflict stress and well-being at work is particularly strong for employees who employ low third-party help as opposed to employees who employ high third-party help.

METHOD

Procedure and participants

A total of 257 employees of two healthcare organizations in the Netherlands were invited to take part in this research and received a questionnaire; 107 of them returned the questionnaire, representing a response rate of 42%. The sample included 103 women and 5 men,[2] with a mean age of 41 years (range = 19 – 60 years). On average, the participants had 18 years of work

---

[2]This women/men ratio, which is highly similar to the actual ratio in both organizations, may be regarded as typical for many healthcare organizations specialized in nursing.

experience, they were in their current job for 8 years, and were employed for 21 hours a week. No response biases were found.

Respondents received a questionnaire that was divided into three subsequent parts. In Part 1, participants reported on conflict styles, followed by some demographical questions in Part 2. Conflict and indicators of well-being were measured in Part 3.

Intrapersonal conflict stress and interpersonal conflict

Conflict stress was measured with four items derived from the Perceived Stress Scale (Cohen, Kamarck, & Mermelstein, 1983) that was specifically adjusted to conflict situations (for items, see Table 1). Also, respondents reported on the frequency of task conflict and relationship conflict with their colleagues (cf. Jehn, 1995; for items see also Table 1). All items were measured on 7-point Likert scales ranging from $1 =$ "never" to $7 =$ "always". The internal consistency of all three scales was good ($\alpha = .90$ for conflict stress, $\alpha = .86$ for task conflict, and $\alpha = .80$ for relationship conflict).

Well-being at work

We included three indicators of well-being at work. *Emotional exhaustion* was assessed using the Dutch version (Schaufeli & Van Dierendonck, 2000) of the Maslach Burnout Inventory—General Survey (Schaufeli, Leiter, Maslach, & Jackson, 1996). This scale consists of five items, such as "I feel mentally exhausted by my work" and "I feel empty after a day's work". All items were measured on 7-point Likert scales ranging from $1 =$ "never" to $7 =$ "always" (Cronbach's alpha is .84). *Absenteeism* was measured by asking respondents to indicate how many days in the past 6 months they were absent from their work. *Turnover intentions* were measured with six items from Hagedoorn, Van Yperen, Van de Vliert, and Buunk (1999). Examples of items are "I am thinking about changing jobs" and "I am actively looking for another job outside this organization". All items were measured on 7-point Likert scales ranging from $1 =$ "totally disagree" to $7 =$ "totally agree" (Cronbach's alpha is .92).

Conflict style

Third-party help was measured with four items (Ting-Toomey & Oetzel, 2001; see Table 2). The items could be rated on 7-point Likert scales ranging from $1 =$ "to a low extent" to $7 =$ "to a high extent" (Cronbach's alpha $= .90$). To be able to examine the relationship between third-party help and four traditional styles of conflict handling (accommodating,

TABLE 1
Results of principal components analysis of conflict stress, task conflict, and relationship conflict

Items	Factors		
	1	2	3
Conflict stress			
How often ...			
do you feel nervous during or directly after a conflict with colleagues?	**.96**	.01	.01
do you become upset during or directly after a conflict with your colleagues?	**.95**	.04	.06
does the stress in a conflict with colleagues increase to such high levels that you cannot let go of it?	**.83**	.09	− .04
do you feel tension during or directly after a conflict with colleagues?	**.82**	− .11	− .10
Task conflict			
How often do you and your colleagues have ...			
divergent ideas on the execution of tasks?	.08	**.89**	.12
different opinions on the organization of work?	.02	**.84**	.01
different visions on work?	− .07	**.78**	− .10
different notions on the cause and solution of work-related problems?	.01	**.74**	− .23
Relationship conflict			
How often are there ...			
emotional conflicts between you and your colleagues?	.02	− .03	− **.89**
controversies between you and your colleagues?	.05	− .07	− **.82**
tensions in the personal field between you and your colleagues?	.01	.11	− **.75**
personal clashes between you and your colleagues?	.01	.36	− **.52**
Eigenvalue	2.44	5.20	1.10
Percentage of variance explained	20.36	43.39	9.14

forcing, avoiding, and problem solving) respondents also filled in the Dutch Test of Conflict Handling (DUTCH; see Van de Vliert, 1997; see also De Dreu, Evers, Beersma, Kluwer, & Nauta, 2001; for items see Table 2). As for third-party help, all items were rated on 7-point Likert scales ranging from 1 = "to a low extent" to 7 = "to a high extent" (Cronbach's alpha varied from .73 to .85).

Social support

We measured social support from the respondents' colleagues as well as from their direct supervisor. Each scale was measured with five items,

TABLE 2
Results of principal components analysis of styles of conflict handling

Items	Factors				
	1	2	3	4	5
Third-party help					
I use a third party to resolve the conflict.	**.86**	.11	.04	.02	.05
I ask a third party to intervene and help us solve our conflict issue.	**.80**	− .12	.03	.03	− .03
I trust a third party to help solve the conflict.	**.79**	.13	.08	.10	− .08
I ask a third party to give us advice on how the conflict issue between myself and the other party can be resolved.	**.86**	.06	− .06	.01	.02
Avoiding					
I avoid a confrontation about our differences.	.13	**.83**	− .10	− .03	− .04
I sidestep a collision with other party.	.12	**.80**	.03	− .06	.07
I bypass our quarrel as much as possible.	− .18	**.75**	.21	− .09	− .03
I attempt to avert contrasts.	.15	**.56**	− .02	− .13	− .32
Forcing					
I fight for a favourable outcome for myself.	.05	.03	**.82**	.04	.02
I struggle for winning our dispute.	− .09	− .08	**.80**	.06	− .05
I try to push through my standpoint.	.04	.08	**.78**	− .06	− .01
I do everything to win.	.01	.07	**.78**	− .06	.01
Problem solving					
I stand up for both my own and the other's goals.	− .05	.07	− .01	**.89**	.07
I work out a decision that meets my own and other's interests.	.08	− .03	.11	**.78**	.07
Together with the other party, I scrutinize the issue till we find an outcome that satisfies both of us.	− .03	− .16	− .06	**.76**	.11
I explore mutual ideas to distil outcomes that are optimal for both of us.	.20	− .10	− .09	**.75**	− .22
Accommodating					
I admit to the ideas of the other party.	.13	− .17	.11	− .14	− **.88**
I indulge in favour of the other party.	− .01	.28	− .19	− .09	− **.72**
I comply with other party's objectives.	− .29	.33	.04	.23	− **.58**
Eigenvalue	3.39	4.61	2.57	1.77	0.96
Percentage of variance explained	17.84	24.24	13.50	9.32	5.08

representing social emotional as well as informational forms of social support (cf. House, 1981; Quick et al., 1997). Examples of the items are "To what extent can you rely on your colleagues (or direct supervisor) to help you out", "To what extent do you get along with your colleagues (or direct supervisor), and "To what extent do you receive good advice from your colleagues (or direct supervisor) about your work". As for conflict management styles, items were rated on 7-point Likert scales ranging from 1 = "to a low extent" to 7 = "to a high extent". Cronbach's alpha was .86 for social support from colleagues and .92 for social support from the respondents' direct supervisor.

RESULTS

Exploratory factor analyses

Before testing the hypotheses, we conducted two exploratory factor analyses in order to get some evidence for the measures' discriminant validity. First, the items of the measures of conflict stress, task conflict, and relationship conflict were submitted to a principal components analysis with oblique rotation. As can be seen in Table 1, three factors emerged accounting for 73% of the variance. Each item loaded on its appropriate factor whereby primary loadings exceeded .52 and cross-loadings were lower than .36. As such, this factor structure provided evidence that respondents distinguished conflict stress from the conflict types of task and relationship conflict.

Second, the items of the five styles of conflict handling (third-party help, accommodating, avoiding, forcing, and problem solving) were factor analysed. As is shown in Table 2, after deleting one item of the accommodating scale ("I give in to the wishes of the other party") which loaded only .22 on the accommodating scale and .57 on the avoiding scale, the five factors emerged appropriately represented the five styles of conflict handling, whereby primary loadings exceeded .56 while cross-loadings were lower than .33. The five factors accounted for 70% of the variance in the items. This factor structure supported our presupposition that the particular conflict handling style of third-party help can be meaningfully distinguished from the classical styles of problem solving, forcing, avoiding, and accommodating (cf. De Dreu et al., 2001).

Descriptive statistics and correlations

Means, standard deviations, and zero-order Pearson correlations among all variables in this study are presented in Table 3. As expected, conflict stress was positively related to both task conflict and relationship conflict. Moreover, conflict stress appeared to be positively correlated to the three indicators of well-being: emotional exhaustion, absenteeism, and turnover intentions. Furthermore, the substantial correlation between task and relationship conflict, $r = .53$, $p < .001$, is in line with prior findings (for an overview, see Simons & Peterson, 2000).

TABLE 3
Univariate statistics and Pearson correlations among the variables ($N = 108$)

Variables	Mean	SD	1	2	3	4	5	6	7	8	9	10	11	12	13	14	15
1. Gender	1.96	0.19															
2. Age	41.16	9.30	.11														
3. Tenure	7.92	6.03	.10	.47													
4. Conflict stress	2.88	1.37	.05	.09	−.03												
5. Task conflict	2.74	0.79	−.27	−.15	.02	.24											
6. Relationship conflict	1.83	0.59	−.06	−.07	.07	.39	.53										
7. Third-party help	3.61	1.33	.01	.08	.11	.07	.09	.08									
8. Accommodating	3.49	0.91	−.01	.03	−.05	.26	.03	.03	.04								
9. Avoiding	3.22	1.18	.03	−.02	−.09	.21	−.02	.01	.18	.62							
10. Forcing	2.77	1.05	−.21	−.24	−.06	.01	.18	.07	.03	.01	.12						
11. Problem solving	4.71	1.23	−.11	−.06	.09	−.24	−.03	−.10	.18	−.23	−.39	−.06					
12. Social support colleagues	5.38	0.99	.19	−.04	−.05	−.10	−.13	−.13	.26	−.22	−.23	−.05	.36				
13. Social support supervisor	5.05	1.49	.11	.07	−.01	−.16	−.20	−.20	.17	−.14	−.13	−.01	.16	.56			
14. Emotional exhaustion	2.57	1.18	−.11	.10	.17	.31	.18	.27	−.13	.14	−.01	−.04	−.14	−.44	−.27		
15. Absenteeism	8.50	23.18	−.03	.10	.03	.17	−.02	−.02	.02	.14	.15	.10	−.04	−.16	.01	.36	
16. Turnover intentions	1.94	1.27	−.15	−.11	.08	.21	.14	.15	−.15	.08	−.06	.10	−.01	−.28	−.28	.50	.27

Correlations above .19 are significant at the .05 level, above .25 at the .01 level (two-sided).

Test of the hypotheses

To test Hypothesis 1 predicting that conflict stress is especially related to relationship conflict, we conducted a multiple regression analysis in order to control for the common variance in task and relationship conflict (see Table 4). In the first step of the analysis, the sociodemographic variables were entered as covariates to control for relationships with conflict stress and conflict type. In the second step, task and relationship conflict were included to test their unique relationships with conflict stress. As expected, conflict stress was found to be positively related to relationship conflict (see Step 2 of the regression equation) but unrelated to task conflict. Thus, we found support for Hypothesis 1.

Furthermore, conflict stress was hypothesized to be positively related to the indicators of individual well-being: emotional exhaustion (H2a), absenteeism (H2b), and turnover intentions (H2c). To test these hypotheses, we conducted hierarchical regression analyses consisting of two steps. The first step included covariates in order to control for the sociodemographics and the conflict types of task and relationship conflict. As shown in Table 5, the second step of the regressions revealed that conflict stress was positively related to emotional exhaustion, absenteeism, and turnover intentions. These results provided full support for Hypotheses 2a, 2b, and 2c.

Finally, to test whether third-party help buffered the positive relationships between conflict stress and individual well-being, hierarchical regression analyses were applied to detect possible interactive effects. These regressions consisted of three steps. After controlling for the sociodemographic variables and conflict type in Step 1 and the main effects of the

TABLE 4
Results of regression analyses of conflict stress on conflict type[a]

	Conflict stress	
Step and variables entered	1	2
1. Gender	.04	.09
Age	.13	.19
Tenure	− .10	− .16
2. Task conflict		.10
Relationship conflict		.37***
R^2 change	.02	.17***
R^2	.02	.19***

[a]Standardized regression coefficients are reported for the respective regression steps including sociodemographics (Step 1) and conflict types (Step 2). $N = 108$. ***$p < .001$, two-tailed significance.

TABLE 5

Results of regression analyses of emotional exhaustion, absenteeism, and turnover intentions on conflict stress and third-party help[a]

Step and variables entered	Emotional exhaustion					Absenteeism					Turnover intentions				
	1a	2a	1b	2b	3b	1a	2a	1b	2b	3b	1a	2a	1b	2b	3b
1. Gender	−.11	−.14	−.13	−.16	−.17	−.04	−.06	−.89	−1.33	−1.50	−.14	−.16	−.17	−.20	−.21
Age	.07	.02	.07	.03	.07	.11	.07	2.50	1.57	2.33	−.16	−.21	−.21	−.25	−.18
Tenure	.13	.17	.16	.22	.15	−.02	.02	−.33	.42	−1.05	.16	.20	.20	.27	.14
Task conflict	.03	−.01	.03	.02	.03	−.01	−.02	−.03	−.53	−.31	.02	.01	.03	.02	.04
Relationship conflict	.25*	.15	.29*	.18	.20	−.02	−.09	−.40	−2.19	−1.90	.11	.02	.13	.03	.05
2. Conflict stress		.26*		.31**	.30*		.21+		4.90+	4.86+		.24*		.31*	.29*
Third-party help				−.22*	−.24*				.16	−.40				−.22	−.27*
3. Conflict stress *Third-party help					−.23*					−4.12+					−.40**
R² change	.11*	.05*	.11*	.09**	.03*	.01	.04+	.01	.04	.03+	.07	.05*	.07*	.08*	.09**
R²	.11*	.16**	.11*	.20**	.23***	.01	.05	.01	.05	.08	.07	.12*	.07	.15*	.23***

[a]Standardized regression coefficients are reported for the regression of emotional exhaustion, absenteeism, and turnover intentions on sociodemographics (Step 1a) and conflict stress (Step 2a). N = 108. Unstandardized regression coefficients are reported for the regression of emotional exhaustion, absenteeism, and turnover intentions on sociodemographics (Step 1b), conflict stress and third-party help (Step 2b), and the interaction of conflict stress and third-party help (Step 3b). N = 108.

+ p < .05, one-tailed significance; * p < .05, two-tailed significance; ** p < .01, two-tailed significance; *** p < .001, two-tailed significance.

predictor variables of conflict stress and third-party help in Step 2, the third step involved the cross-product term of conflict stress and third-party help in order to detect interactive effects. To minimize problems of multicollinearity and facilitate interpretation, the predictor variables were standardized before calculation of the cross-product term and regression statistics (Aiken & West, 1991). The analyses showed that conflict stress and third-party help did indeed interact in their effects on emotional exhaustion, R^2-change = .03, $b = -.23$, $p < .05$, absenteeism, R^2-change = .03, $b = -4.42$, $p < .05$, one-tailed significance, and turnover intentions, R^2-change = .08, $b = -.40$, $p < .001$.

To interpret these interaction effects, the total regression equations were rearranged into simple regressions of the outcome variables on conflict stress given conditional values of third-party help ($M + 1SD$; $M - 1SD$) (cf. Aiken & West, 1991). As shown in Figure 1, in the case of high levels of third-party help, conflict stress was unrelated to emotional exhaustion, $b = .07$, ns, absenteeism, $b = .26$, ns, and turnover intentions, $b = -.11$, ns. However, at low levels of third-party help, conflict stress appeared to have positive relationships with emotional exhaustion, $b = .53$, $p < .001$, absenteeism, $b = 9.10$, $p < .01$, and turnover intentions, $b = .69$, $p < .001$. These findings signify that conflict stress and third-party help interacted in their effects in such a way that high levels of third-party help were needed to buffer the detrimental effects of conflict stress on individual well-being. These results supported Hypothesis 3.

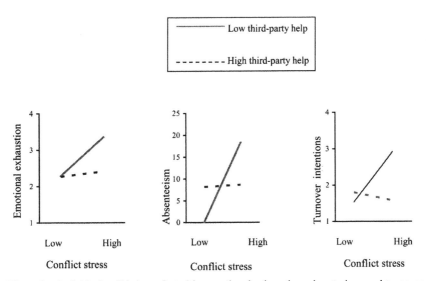

Figure 1. Individual well-being reflected by emotional exhaustion, absenteeism, and turnover intentions predicted by the two-way interaction between conflict stress and third-party help.

Supplementary analyses

As noted in the theoretical section, conflict parties might receive social support from colleagues or supervisors and experience this support as third-party help. As such, social support from colleagues or supervisors might be responsible for the moderating effect of third-party help in the relationships between conflict stress and individual well-being. To rule out this alternative explanation, we repeated the series of regression analyses reported in which the interactive effects of conflict stress and third-party help were controlled for two sources of social support, namely support from colleagues and support from supervisors. After controlling for social support, sociodemographics, and type of conflict (Step 1), and the main effects of conflict stress and third-party help (Step 2), the interaction effect between conflict stress and third-party help (Step 3) remained significant for emotional exhaustion, R^2-change = .03, $b = -.23$, $p < .05$, absenteeism, R^2-change = .04, $b = -5.78$, $p < .05$, and turnover intentions, R^2-change = .07, $b = -.38$, $p < .01$. These results contradict the alternative explanation that the moderating effect of third-party help can be ascribed to social support.

Finally, we conducted supplementary regression analyses to test whether conflict stress interacted with the conflict handling styles of problem solving, forcing, accommodating, and avoiding in its effects on the outcome variables. As such, separate regression analyses were applied to detect possible interactive effects of conflict stress and each of the different conflict handling styles. No significant interaction effects were found. So, third-party help appeared to be exclusive in buffering the positive relationships between conflict stress and individual well-being in terms of emotional exhaustion, absenteeism, and turnover intentions.

DISCUSSION

The purpose of the current study was to examine the potential detrimental consequences of conflict at work for individual well-being and to examine the possible buffering effect of third-party help. We proposed that particularly the stress directly associated with conflict at work is responsible for reduced individual well-being of employees. Our analyses showed that conflict stress could be meaningfully distinguished from relationship conflict and task conflict, and that both types of conflict correlated with conflict stress. Additional regression analyses showed that the relationship between task conflict and conflict stress disappeared when controlled for relationship conflict. Thus, as expected, particularly relationship conflict leads to feelings of tension and stress, probably because it threatens one's social identity and self-esteem to a greater extent than task conflict. Further analyses show a relatively high correlation between relationship and task conflict. A meta-analytical study by Simons and Peterson (2000) found that when correlations between both types of conflict are relatively high, within-team trust is usually low. Especially in low trusting environments, one might expect a particularly strong bond between the occurrence of conflict and feelings of tension and stress. Thus, the question is whether our expectations would also receive support in high trusting environments.

Furthermore, we argued that heightened levels of conflict stress hinder individuals to process and exchange information (cf. De Dreu & Weingart, 2003). As a consequence, conflict intensifies and parties are likely to engage in destructive conflict spirals ultimately leading to reduced individual well-being. In line with this reasoning, we found that conflict stress was significantly related to all three indicators of deteriorated individual well-being included in this study: emotional exhaustion, absenteeism, and turnover intentions. Departing from the assumption that inaccurate information processing lies at the heart of ill-handled conflict, third-party help may block conflict escalation processes in several ways. As argued, third parties may simply promote more thorough and accurate information processing within the conflicting parties themselves (Volkema et al., 1996), for example by asking critical questions. Additionally, third parties may provide concrete input, for example by suggesting alternative solutions the conflicting parties had not thought of themselves. Both lines of reasoning are supported by previous research showing that third-party help leads to better quality solutions (Karambayya & Brett, 1989; Karambayya et al., 1992; Lewicki & Sheppard, 1985).

Another explanation may be that the involvement of a third party renders a greater acceptance of possible solutions by the conflicting parties, even when the absolute quality of the solution does not improve. The reason for this may be that the process resulting from third-party help may be seen as more procedurally just and fair than other conflict management strategies (cf. Karambayya & Brett, 1989). In line with research stressing that injustice perceptions foster destructive responses (Van Yperen, Hagedoorn, Zweers, & Postma, 2000), process and relational aspects of involving third-party help may be of high importance as well. Support for this also comes from cross-cultural research, suggesting that in cultures where confrontational strategies are less common and relational concerns play an important role, third-party help is used effectively to help both parties save face (Kozan & Ilter, 1994; Ting-Toomey & Oetzel, 2001). Future research might examine these alternative explanations in light of their consequences for both individual well-being and performance, preferably in a cross-cultural context.

Although we found no direct support for one or more of the underlying processes explaining our findings, we could rule out the alternative explanation that conflict parties might receive social support from colleagues or supervisors and experience this support as third-party help. Remember that our results did not change after controlling for social support from colleagues and direct supervisors. Thus, perceived social support should be regarded conceptually different from third-party help, because it reflects a person's generalized cognitive appraisal of being supported rather than enacted behaviours *per se* (Lakey & Cassady, 1990; Thompson-Ross, Lutz, & Lakey, 1999). Our study shows that third-party help may be seen as an additional conflict-handling style (cf. Ting-Toomey & Oetzel, 2001), and that employees differ in their preference for third-party help.

Despite the fact that social support and third-party help may be regarded two separate constructs, correlations in Table 1 show that third-party help is moderately, yet significantly, associated with perceived social support by colleagues, and not with social support by the direct supervisor. This may shed some light on what kind of third party is chosen and preferred. Considering that the organizations in our study did not employ a corporate ombudsman and conflict parties thus seem to have the choice between the more informal interventions of supervisors or colleagues, parties may prefer and use the latter more. Yet, both peers and supervisors usually have no official mediation function or credentials (Arnold & O'Connor, 1999). Because an increasing number of organizations employ a corporate ombudsman to mediate in conflict situations, additional research is needed to look into preferences for different types of third parties. This is particularly important since research shows that the type of interventions by informal parties differ substantially from the type of interventions made by more formal third parties (Pinkley et al., 1995), and that dispute resolution strategies differ across cultures (cf. Tinsley, 2004).

There were several shortcomings to the present study. Firstly, the reliance on self-report measures may be considered a limitation of the current study. The link between conflict stress and indicators of individual well-being may be the result of common method variance. This may be particularly true for emotional exhaustion, which can be considered a measure for long-term stress. Yet, similar patterns for the relatively "objective" measure of absenteeism, in terms of the number of days one is absent from work, as well as for turnover intentions point at the robustness of the relations found. Another limitation of the current study is that the relationships are correlational and not causal. Thus, theoretically, conflict may be a consequence of deteriorated well-being (De Dreu et al., 2002), rather than the reverse. Perhaps reduced well-being of employees deteriorates interpersonal relationships and thus increases the likelihood of conflicts with others. Finally, this study's findings are primarily based on the responses of female employees, who reported on conflicts with co-workers. Male employees might experience and handle conflict differently, and hierarchical conflicts with either subordinates or supervisors may elicit different processes (cf. Frone, 2000).

In sum, the data confirm our expectation that conflict, and especially the tension and stress directly associated with it, threatens individual well-being. Since conflict is an unavoidable consequence of organizational life, research should focus on conditions that may buffer its negative consequences. Our study shows that the conflict management style of third-party help may be considered such a condition.

REFERENCES

Aiken, L. S., & West, S. G. (1991). *Multiple regression: Testing and interpreting interactions*. Newbury Park, CA: Sage.

Amason, A. C. (1996). Distinguishing the effects of functional and dysfunctional conflict on strategic decision making: Resolving a paradox for top management groups. *Academy of Management Journal, 39*, 123–148.

Arnold, J. A., & O'Connor, K. M. (1999). Ombudspersons or peers? The effects of third-party expertise and recommendations on negotiation. *Journal of Applied Psychology, 84*, 776–785.

Bakker, A. B., Schaufeli, W. B., Sixma, H., Bosveld, W., & Van Dierendonck, D. (2000). Patient demands, lack of reciprocity, and burnout: A five-year longitudinal study among general practitioners. *Journal of Organizational Behavior, 21*, 425–441.

Baumeister, R. F., & Leary, M. R. (1995). The need to belong: Desire for interpersonal attachments as a fundamental human motivation. *Psychological Bulletin, 117*, 497–529.

Brown, L. D. (1983). *Managing conflict at organizational interfaces*. Reading, MA: Addison-Wesley.

Cohen, S., Kamarck, T., & Mermelstein, R. (1983). A global measure of perceived stress. *Journal of Health and Social Behavior, 24*, 385–396.

Cohen, S., & Wills, T. A. (1985). Stress, social support, and the buffering hypothesis. *Psychological Bulletin, 98*, 310–357.

Conlon, D. E., & Ross, W. H. (1993). The effects of partisan third parties on negotiator behavior and outcome perceptions. *Journal of Applied Psychology, 78*, 280–290.

Cropanzano, R., Rupp, D. E., & Byrne, Z. S. (2003). The relationship of emotional exhaustion to work attitudes, job performance, and organizational citizenship behaviors. *Journal of Applied Psychology, 88*, 160–169.

De Dreu, C. K. W., Evers, A., Beersma, B., Kluwer, E. S., & Nauta, A. (2001). A theory-based measure of conflict management strategies in the work place. *Journal of Organizational Behavior, 22*, 645–668.

De Dreu, C. K. W., Giebels, E., & Van de Vliert, E. (1998). Social motives and trust in integrative negotiation: The disruptive effects of punitive capability. *Journal of Applied Psychology, 83*, 408–422.

De Dreu, C. K. W., Harinck, F., & Van Vianen, A. E. M. (1999). Conflict and performance in groups and organizations. In C. L. Cooper & I. T. Robertson (Eds.), *International review of industrial and organizational psychology* (pp. 376–405). Chichester, UK: Wiley.

De Dreu, C. K. W., & Van de Vliert, E. (Eds.). (1997). *Using conflict in organizations*. London: Sage.

De Dreu, C. K. W., Van Dierendonck, D., & De Best-Waldhober, M. (2002). Conflict at work and individual wellbeing. In M. Schabracq, J. A. M. Winnubst, & C. L. Cooper (Eds.), *The handbook of work and health psychology*. Chichester, UK: Wiley.

De Dreu, C. K. W., & Weingart, L. R. (2003). Task versus relationship conflict, team performance and team member satisfaction: A meta-analysis. *Journal of Applied Psychology*, *88*, 741–749.

Elangovan, A. R. (1995). Managerial third-party dispute intervention: A prescriptive model of strategy selection. *Academy of Management Review*, *20*, 800–830.

Fiske, A. P. (1992). The four elementary forms of sociability: Framework for a unified theory of social relations. *Psychological Review*, *99*, 689–723.

Frone, M. R. (2000). Interpersonal conflict at work and psychological outcomes: Testing a model among young workers. *Journal of Occupational Health Psychology*, *5*, 246–255.

Giebels, E., De Dreu, C. K. W., & Van de Vliert, E. (2000). Interdependence in negotiation: Effects of exit options and social motive on distributive and integrative negotiation. *European Journal of Social Psychology*, *30*, 255–272.

Greenglass, E. R., Fiksenbaum, L., & Burke, R. J. (1994). The relationship between social support and burnout over time in teachers. *Journal of Social Behavior and Personality*, *9*, 219–230.

Hagedoorn, M., van Yperen, N. W., Van de Vliert, E., & Buunk, B. P. (1999). Employees' reactions to problematic events: A circumplex structure of five categories of responses, and the role of job satisfaction. *Journal of Organizational Behavior*, *20*, 309–321.

Hardy, G. E., Woods, D., & Wall, T. D. (2003). The impact of psychological distress on absence from work. *Journal of Applied Psychology*, *88*, 306–314.

Heuven, E., & Bakker, A. B. (2003). Emotional dissonance and burnout among cabin attendants. *Journal of Work and Organizational Psychology*, *12*, 81–100.

House, J. S. (1981). *Work stress and social support*. Reading, MA: Addison-Wesley.

Janssen, O., Van de Vliert, E., & Veenstra, C. (1999). How task and person conflict shape the role of positive interdependence in management teams. *Journal of Management*, *25*, 117–142.

Jehn, K. (1995). A multimethod examination of the benefits and detriments of intragroup conflict. *Administrative Science Quarterly*, *40*, 256–282.

Jex, S. M. (1998). *Occupational stress and job performance*. Thousand Oaks, CA: Sage.

Karambayya, R., & Brett, J. M. (1989). Managers handling disputes: Third-party roles and perceptions of fairness. *Academy of Management Journal*, *32*, 687–704.

Karambayya, R., Brett, J. M. & Lytle, A. (1992). Effects of formal authority and experience on third-party roles, outcomes, and perceptions of fairness. *Academy of Management Journal*, *35*, 426–438.

Keenan, A., & Newton, T. J. (1985). Stressful events, stressors, and psychological strains in young professional engineers. *Journal of Occupational Behavior*, *6*, 151–156.

Kolb, D. M. (1986). Who are organizational third parties and what do they do? In R. J. Lewicki, B. H. Sheppard, & M. H. Bazerman (Eds.), *Research on negotiation in organizations* (Vol. 1, pp. 207–228). Greenwich, CT: JAI Press.

Kozan, M. K., & Ilter, S. S. (1994). Third-party roles played by Turkish managers in subordinates' conflicts. *Journal of Organizational Behavior*, *15*, 453–466.

Lakey, B., & Cassady, P. B. (1990). Cognitive processes in perceived social support. *Journal of Personality and Social Psychology*, *59*, 337–343.

Lee, R. T., & Ashforth, B. E. (1996). A meta-analytic examination of the correlates of the three dimensions of burnout. *Journal of Applied Psychology*, *81*, 123–133.

Lewicki, R. J., & Sheppard, B. H. (1985). Choosing how to intervene: Factors affecting the use of process and outcome control in third-party resolution. *Journal of Occupational Behavior*, *6*, 49–64.

Maslach, C. (1982). *Burnout: The cost of caring.* Englewood Cliffs, NJ: Prentice Hall.

Pines, T. L., & Aronson, E. (1988). *Career burnout: Causes and cures.* New York: Free Press.

Pinkley, R. L., Neale, M. A., Brittain, J., & Northcraft, G. B. (1995). Managerial third-party dispute intervention: An inductive analysis of intervenor strategy selection. *Journal of Applied Psychology, 80,* 386–402.

Quick, J. C., Quick, J. D., Nelson, D. L., & Hurrell, J. J. (1997). *Preventive stress management in organizations* (2nd ed.). Washington, DC: American Psychological Association.

Schaufeli, W. B., & Van Dierendonck, D. (2000). *De UBOS, Utrechtse Burnout Schaal, handleiding* [UBOS: Utrecht Burnout Scale—manual]. Utrecht, The Netherlands: Swets Test Services.

Schaufeli, W. B., Leiter, M. P., Maslach, C., & Jackson, S. E. (1996). The Maslach Burnout Inventory—general survey. In C. Maslach, S. E. Jackson, & M. P. Leiter (Eds.), *Maslach Burnout Inventory—manual* (3rd ed.). Palo Alto, CA: Consulting Psychologists Press.

Sheppard, B. H. (1984). Third party intervention: A procedural framework. In B. Staw & L. Cummings (Eds.), *Research on negotiation in organizations* (Vol. 6, pp. 114–137). Greenwich, CT: JAI Press.

Shirom, A. (1989). Burnout in work organizations. In C. L. Cooper & I. T. Robertson (Eds.), *International review of industrial and organizational psychology* (pp. 25–48). New York: Wiley.

Simons, T. L., & Peterson, R. S. (2000). Task conflict and relationship conflict in top management teams: The pivotal role of intragroup trust. *Journal of Applied Psychology, 85,* 102–111.

Spector, P. E., & Jex, S. M. (1998). Development of four self-report measures of job stressors and strains: Interpersonal conflict at work scale, organizational constraints scale, quantitative workload inventory, and physical symptoms inventory. *Journal of Occupational Health Psychology, 3,* 356–367.

Sutton, R. I., & Kahn, R. L. (1987). Predicting, understanding, and control as antidotes to organizational stress. In J. W. Lorrsch (Ed.), *Handbook of organizational behavior* (pp. 272–285). Englewood Cliffs, NJ: Prentice-Hall.

Thomson-Ross, L., Lutz, C. J., & Lakey, B. (1999). Perceived social support and attributions for failed support. *Personality and Social Psychology Bulletin, 25,* 896–908.

Ting-Toomey, S., & Oetzel, J. G. (2001). *Managing intercultural conflict effectively.* Thousand Oaks, CA: Sage.

Ting-Toomey, S., Yee-Jung, K., Shapiro, R., Garcia, W., Wright, T., & Oetzel, J. G. (2000). Cultural/ethnic identity salience and conflict styles in four U.S. ethnic groups. *International Journal of Intercultural Relations, 24,* 47–81.

Tinsley, C. (2004). Culture and conflict: Enlarging our dispute resolution framework. In M. J. Gelfand & J. M. Brett (Eds.), *The handbook of negotiation and culture* (pp. 193–210). Palo Alto, CA: Stanford University Press.

Van de Vliert, E. (1997). *Complex interpersonal conflict behaviour.* Hove, UK: Psychology Press.

Van Yperen, N. W., Hagedoorn, M., Zweers, M., & Postma, S. (2000). Injustice and employees' destructive responses: The mediating role of state negative affect. *Social Justice Research, 13,* 291–312.

Volkema, R. J., Farquhar, K., & Bergmann, T. J. (1996). Third-party sensemaking in interpersonal conflicts at work: A theoretical framework. *Human Relations, 49,* 1437–1454.

Wall, J., & Callister, R. (1995). Conflicts and its management. *Journal of Management, 21,* 515–558.

Wright, T. A., & Cropanzano, R. (1998). Emotional exhaustion as a predictor of job performance and voluntary turnover. *Journal of Applied Psychology, 83,* 486–493.

EUROPEAN JOURNAL OF WORK AND
ORGANIZATIONAL PSYCHOLOGY
2005, 14 (2), 157–176

Ψ Psychology Press
Taylor & Francis Group

A contingency perspective on the study of the consequences of conflict types: The role of organizational culture

José M. Guerra

University of San Pablo-CEU, Seville, Spain

Inés Martínez

University of Pablo de Olavide, Seville, Spain

Lourdes Munduate and Francisco J. Medina

University of Seville, Spain

The potential positive or negative consequence of relationship conflict versus task conflict for group members and organizations continues to be a controversial topic. Whereas a certain amount of agreement exists on the negative consequences of relationship conflict, the evidence for task conflict is not as conclusive. This has led some authors (De Dreu & Weingart, 2003a, 2003b) to propose a contingency perspective. This article continues this approach and analyses the influence of types of conflict on group members' satisfaction and well-being, considering the moderating role that organizational culture plays in this relationship. Two types of service organization have been studied: private organizations with a high goal-oriented culture, and public organizations with a low goal-oriented culture. Results show that (a) relationship conflict decreases both public and private workers' job satisfaction and affective well-being; (b) task conflicts decrease private organization workers' satisfaction and affective well-being, while this dysfunctional effect is absent in public organizations; (c) goal orientation culture moderates the effect of task conflict in private organizations; and (d) support orientation culture moderates the effect of task conflict in public organizations.

Correspondence should be addressed to Francisco J. Medina, Department of Social Psychology, Facultad de Ciencias del Trabajo, University of Seville, Madre de Dios, 1, 41004, Sevilla, Spain. Email: fjmedina@us.es

The authors would like to thank Carsten de Dreu and Bianca Beersma for their helpful comments on an early version of this manuscript.

http://www.tandf.co.uk/journals/pp/1359432X.html   DOI: 10.1080/13594320444000245

The study of the consequences of conflict in organizational settings is ongoing (Thomas, 1992). Early organizational conflict theorists suggested that conflict is detrimental to organizational functioning (e.g., Pondy, 1967). In contrast, more recent studies have demonstrated that conflict can be beneficial, so that it might even be recommended to stimulate conflict (Amason, 1996; Jehn, 1994; Van de Vliert & De Dreu, 1994). Some studies show that on certain occasions, conflict may increase creativity and job quality in a group (e.g., Amason, 1996; Nemeth, 1986), and improve organizational effectiveness and development (Bourgeois, 1985; Eisenhardt & Schoonhoven, 1990). However, conclusions about the positive consequences of stimulating conflict are not conclusive. Authors such as De Dreu, Harinck, and Van Vianen (1999) have considered four factors that may moderate the results of conflict stimulation: (a) *conflict experience*, referring to feelings, cognitions, and intentions associated to conflict; (b) *conflict management*, understood as those behaviours or set of behaviours aimed at the intensification, reduction, or resolution of the conflict; (c) *conflict results*, understood as the extent to which an agreement is reached, and the quality of this agreement; and (d) *types of conflict*, understood as the specific issues that give rise to arguments. This article analyses the influence of this final factor, conflict types, on the affective reactions of group members.

TYPES OF CONFLICT AND PERSONAL AND ORGANIZATIONAL CONSEQUENCES

The positive or negative consequences of conflict types for group members and for the organization itself have been the object of much research in recent years (e.g., De Dreu & Weingart, 2003b). However, results are still far from conclusive. Following the classic research by Guetzkow and Gyr (1954) most research has considered the existence of two types of conflict: that based on the interpersonal relationships within the group, and that based around tasks developed by the group (e.g., Amason & Schweiger, 1994; Jehn, 1995; Pinkley, 1990). *Relationship conflicts* are disagreements and incompatibilities among group members over personal issues that are not task related. The most frequently reported relationship conflicts concern social events, gossip, clothing preferences, political views, and hobbies (Jehn, 1997). This type of conflict often includes personality differences, animosity, and annoyance between individuals. In contrast, *task conflicts* are disagreements among group members or individuals about the content of the task being performed, including differences in viewpoints, ideas, and opinions. Examples of task conflict are conflicts about the distribution of resources, about procedures or guidelines, and about the interpretation of facts (Jehn, 1995, 1997).

Some research has shown that the two conflict types have different consequences for personal, group, and organizational dynamics. The existence of relationship conflict within the group produces negative emotional reactions in workers such as anxiety, fear, mistrust, or resentment (Jehn, 1995). High relationship conflict also means that workers suffer frustration, tension, and fear of being rejected by other group members (Murnigham & Conlon, 1991). At the same time, high relationship conflict appears to cause dysfunction in the group work, diminish group decision commitment, decrease organizational commitment (Jehn, Northcraft, & Neale, 1999), raise communication problems within team members (Baron, 1991), diminish work satisfaction (Jehn, 1995; Jehn, Chadwick, & Thatcher, 1997), and increase stress levels (Friedman, Tidd, Currall, & Tsai, 2000).

Findings concerning task conflict are not conclusive. Task conflict has usually been associated with several beneficial effects in the group and organizational settings. Task conflict is related to the quality of ideas and innovation (Amason, 1996; West & Anderson, 1996); it increases constructive debate (Jehn et al., 1999), facilitates a more effective use of resources, and leads to better service provision (Tjosvold, Dann, & Wong, 1992). Team members respond positively to decision processes that are open to them, and that consider their needs and concerns (Korsgaard, Schweiger, & Sapienza, 1995) and a greater desire to remain in the group (Amason, 1996). However, other studies have shown that task conflict may also have harmful effects. Conflict in any form can be an uncomfortable environment, decreasing individuals' perceptions of teamwork and their satisfaction (Kabanoff, 1991; Jehn et al., 1997), and increasing their anxiety (Jehn, 1997) and propensity to leave the group (Jehn, 1995).

To analyse the controversial role of task conflict, De Dreu and Weingart (2003b) performed a meta-analysis of research into the associations between relationship conflict, task conflict, team performance, and team member satisfaction. Results revealed that task conflict can be as harmful as relationship conflict for team performance, and team members' satisfaction. These authors also found that task conflict may be moderated by the type of task being performed by subjects, and by work team culture. As a result, and as Jehn (1997) suggested, De Dreu and Weingart point to the possibility of considering a contingent perspective in the study of conflict types outcomes. Following this line of research, the objective of this article is to analyse the effect of conflict types, considering the moderating role played by certain variables in the social context in which these conflicts arise.

When analysing the effects of conflict types, we pay special attention to the effects on employees' emotional reactions, such as satisfaction and well-being. The reason for highlighting these variables is, as different authors have suggested, mainly due to the fact that conflict may have serious consequences for individual well-being and health, and because well-being and satisfaction are important predictors of performance, propensity to leave the job and organizational health (e.g., Spector & Jex, 1998). In addition, the importance of considering these variables is based on the fact that previous research on conflict and individual well-being did not consider the distinction between task and relationship conflict (De Dreu & Weingart, 2003a).

THE MODERATING ROLE OF ORGANIZATIONAL CULTURE

Several authors have argued that organizational culture may render members of a group to be more or less tolerant towards discussions and different opinions that may arise within the group (De Dreu & Weingart, 2003b). Organizational culture is defined in terms of "core values, behavioral norms, artifacts, and behavioral patterns, which govern the ways people in an organization interact with each other and invest energy in their jobs and the organization at large" (Van Muijen, Koopman, Dondeyne, De Cock, & De Witte, 1992, p. 555). This definition has been adopted by its authors following the competing values model of organizational culture (Quinn, 1988). The model consists of two dimensions with contrasting poles. The first dimension represents the organization's point of view. The focus can either be direct internally—making the organization itself, its processes, or its people, the central issue—or externally—making the relation of the organization with its environment the central issue. The second dimension refers to the contrasting pole of flexibility and control. Combining these two dimensions, four organizational culture orientations are obtained: support, innovation, rules, and goal orientation (Quinn, 1988). Organizations can score high on none, one, or any combination of the orientations, thereby showing the level of strength of their culture.

Van Muijen et al. (1999) describe the four different orientations in terms of their related concepts. The support orientation, which combines the internal and flexibility poles, deals with concepts such as participation, cooperation, people-based orientation, mutual trust, team spirit, and individual growth. The innovation orientation (external and flexibility poles) is characterized by concepts such as searching for new information in the environment, creativity, openness to change, anticipation, and experimentation. The rules orientation (internal and control poles) emphasizes respect for authority, rationality of procedures, and division of work. Finally, the goal orientation (external and control poles) emphasizes concepts such as rationality, performance indicators, accomplishment, accountability, and contingent reward.

Van Muijen and Koopman (1994) point out that the orientations are circumflex and as a result there is tension between the values of the diametrical orientations. When one moves diagonally in the model, the culture type is the polar opposite. Stability and control (rules orientation) are opposed to creativity and change (innovation orientation). Team spirit and cooperation (support orientation) contrast with contingent reward and accountability (goal orientation). Our review of the task conflict studies further suggests that these cultural orientations would moderate the consequences of the task conflicts developing within them. However, given the consistency of findings on the relationship conflict, one would not expect them to be affected by the differences in their respective organizational cultures. Exploring these possibilities was the major goal of our study. We compare these effects of task versus relationship conflict in two culturally distinct organizations, a private service organization and a public service organization. Perry and Rainey (1988) have proposed a classification of types of organizations, suggesting that the public and the private (for-profit) forms of organization represent the most distinct types of organizations. For the purposes of this article, we focus on these pure types of organizations.

Private service organizations have a simple structure with two hierarchical levels, management and workers (Mintzberg, 1979). In these organizations work is performed on the basis of criteria of rationality, accomplishment, and accountability with the objective of satisfying clients' needs and obtaining a profit. This type of management assumes the existence of certain clear objectives that guide the organization and working procedures, and a reward system that depends on the performance of its employees. When a high goal orientation culture exists in private organizations, disagreements between employees on how to perform a task—task conflict—may be considered as an essential part of the process and a way of improving work and obtaining profits (Jehn et al., 1999). Therefore, it is possible that task conflict is not negative for group objectives or for the affective well-being of its members. In other words, high job satisfaction and high affective well-being could be achieved when task conflict occurs within a culture that values rationality, accomplishment, and accountability.

Hypothesis 1: Relationship conflict will be negatively related to satisfaction and well-being of private organization employees.

Hypothesis 2: The stronger the goal orientation culture in private organizations, the less negative the relationship between task conflict on the one hand, and satisfaction and well-being on the other.

Public service organizations have a different finality, which consists of providing a service to the general public (Porter, Lawler, & Hackman, 1975). These organizations do not have to compete for clients as is the case with private organizations, they are not driven by the goal of profit making, as their basic remit is to provide a public service to specific groups. These organizations are, to use Mintzberg's (1979) terminology, professional bureaucracies in which the yardstick with which work is assessed is not determined so much by results, organizational criteria or management decisions, as by rules and legally established indications. They combine hierarchical administration with a peer philosophy that views employees as self-governing colleagues, a tenure system for job security, and decentralized departments that often operate independently rather than as part of an organization. In terms of cultural orientation they are a long way from performance indicators, accountability, and contingent rewards.

There are differences in human resources practices in private and public organizations. For example, in a public organization, managers have less discretion in exercising leadership than in private organizations, because responsibilities are clearly specified, authority and accountability are documented in policies, procedures, and job descriptions, and remuneration does not depend on leader recommendations (Hooijberg & Choi, 2001). Moreover, public organizations have less flexibility in their reward systems, more specialized and invariant job designs, higher levels of accountability, more rules and regulations, weaker linkages between political leaders and career-level leaders, and an absence of market incentives (Robertson & Seneviratne, 1995). As a consequence, the effects of task conflict in this context might be distinct to private organizations. Public sector workers have to deal with frequently changing agendas and unstable coalitions (Ring & Perry, 1985). Moreover, as Denhardt (1984) suggests, public employees should have different skills from private organizations: to encourage collective effort, to build cohesion and teamwork, to develop people through a caring and empathetic orientation. In this organizations manager and colleagues have to be helpful, considerate, sensitive, open, approachable, and fair (Denhardt, 1984). The culture orientation that describes largely these skills is the support orientation (Hooijberg & Choi, 2001). We suppose that when a high support orientation exists in public organizations, disagreements between employees on how to perform a task—task conflict—may be considered as differences in interpretation of rules and procedures or as a way of improving the work. In this sense, some authors have pointed out that in groups where there is mutual collaboration and trust, arguments about working procedures are less likely to lead to conflicts on personal matters (Simons & Peterson, 2000). As a result, it is possible that when a high support orientation prevails within a group of a public organization, task conflict will not harm the satisfaction and affective well-being of group members. However, task conflict will have negative consequences on the satisfaction and affective well-being of workers when they perceive a low support culture in their work groups.

Hypothesis 3: Relationship conflict will be negatively related with public organization workers' job satisfaction and affective well-being.

Hypothesis 4: The stronger the support orientation in public service organizations the less negative the relationship between task conflict on the one hand, and satisfaction and affective well-being on the other.

METHOD

Study participants

Data from private organizations were collected from several small/medium-sized hotels. Respondents consisted of 79 men, 86 women, and 4 respondents whose gender was not specified. Subjects had different educational levels: elementary school ($N = 64$), high school ($N = 41$), high school graduates ($N = 41$), and university graduates ($N = 14$). Nine respondents did not indicate their educational level. Work experience ranged from 3 months to more than 5 years, and the average age was 31.45. Data from public organizations were collected at several small/medium homes for senior citizens. Respondents from public organizations consisted of 203 women, 107 men, and 17 respondents whose gender was not specified. Subjects had different educational levels: elementary school ($N = 107$), high school ($N = 166$), high school graduates ($N = 50$), and university graduates ($N = 21$). Work experience ranged from 3 months to more than 5 years, and the average age was 39.

Data collection

Variables were measured using a questionnaire. A cover letter explaining the purpose of the study accompanied the questionnaire. Subjects were told that they would be entitled to a free summary report of the study if they returned the completed questionnaire. They were told that the questionnaire was not designed for their superiors or heads of department, but for their immediate superiors. A researcher was present when they filled out the questionnaire to clarify any doubts. To ensure confidentiality, participants put the completed questionnaire in a sealed box. The response rate was 60%.

Measures

Task and relationship conflict. Jehn's (1995) four-item scale was used to assess *task conflict*. The scale asks respondents to consider the amount of task or work-based conflict he or she experiences with others in the work place (e.g., "How often do people you work with have different opinions about the work being done?"). Each item was cast on a 5-point scale. The higher the score, the higher the level of task conflict experienced.

To measure *relationship conflict* we relied on Cox's (1998) Organizational Conflict Scale. Cox's scale focuses on the active hostility found in relationship conflict and is based on items such as "Much plotting takes place behind the scenes" and "One party frequently undermines the other". We used this scale because it deals more with perceptions of active conflict behaviours rather than perceptions of an overall state of conflict (see Friedman et al., 2001). The scale has a 5-point response format. The higher the score, the higher the levels of relationship conflict experienced.

Organizational culture. To measure organizational culture we used the 40-item adapted version of FOCUS-93 questionnaire (Mañas, González-Romá, & Peiró, 1999; Van Muijen et al., 1999). Respondents were asked to think about all the people with whom they have a working relationship. The questionnaire has two formats. The first format asks subjects how frequently certain situations occur in their workplace (6 items) (e.g., "How often is constructive criticism accepted?") and the second format asks subjects about the number of people in the organization that are affected by certain situations (34 items) (e.g., "How many people with personal problems are helped?"). Subjects answer using a 6-point scale (1 = nobody to 6 = everybody for the first format and 1 = never to 6 = always for the second format). The higher the score, the higher the level of each orientation: support (e.g., "How many people who wish to advance are supported by their superiors?"), innovation (e.g., "How often is there a lot of investment in new products?"), rules (e.g., "How often are written instructions given?"), and goals (e.g., "How often do rewards depend on performance?"). The higher the scores for the total scale, the higher the organizational culture.

Job satisfaction. We measured job satisfaction with the 23-item version of Meliá and Peiró's (1989) Job Satisfaction Scale. Respondents were asked to consider how satisfied they were with intrinsic job aspects, supervision, participation, environment, and services (e.g., "Personal relationships with your superior"). In this study, we used an overall job satisfaction index. The higher the score, the more satisfied the workers.

Affective well-being. Affective well-being was assessed using the scales developed by Warr (1990). The 6-item, 6-point scales measure the extent to which people are either anxious or calm, depressed or enthusiastic, and contented or discontented with their job. Respondents were asked to think of the past few weeks and to indicate how they felt (e.g., "calm", "gloomy", "cheerful", "contented"). Higher scores on these scales are held to represent higher levels of affective well-being.

RESULTS

Table 1 provides for all variables the number of items, means, standard deviations, and internal consistency (Cronbach's alpha). The reliability coefficients for all the variables were generally satisfactory except for the rules scale, which also had an originally low coefficient (.58).

Before testing our hypotheses, we examined whether public organizations were different from private organizations in terms of their level of conflict and their organizational culture. Workers in public organizations perceived higher levels of task conflict, $F(1, 513) = 7.26$, $p < .01$, and more relationship conflict, $F(1, 513) = 19.6$, $p < .01$, than workers in private organizations. Workers in private organizations perceived more support for innovation $F(1, 513) = 123.8$, $p < .01$, goals orientation $F(1, 513) = 73.03$, $p < .01$, and rules orientation $F(1, 513) = 10.20$, $p < .01$, than public organizations. No differences were found in support orientation, $F(1, 513) = 1.99$, ns. Data suggest that there are significant differences in cultural orientations between private and public organizations and that these differences are coherent with our theoretical framework. In effect, private organizations have a more goal, innovation, and rules culture orientation than public organizations, given the need of the latter to adapt to the surroundings and meet demands to survive in these surroundings. In general, it is clear that private organizations have a stronger culture than public organizations, with the exception of support orientation, which deals with peer philosophy, mutual trust, team spirit, and individual growth.

In Table 1 it can be seen that in both public and private organizations, relationship conflict is negatively related with all culture orientations, as well as job satisfaction and affective well-being. In task conflict, differences exist between public and private organizations. In private organizations there are no significant relations between task conflict and culture orientations. However, in public organizations, task conflict is negatively related with all culture orientations except innovation orientation in which case the relation is not significant.

Four multiple regression analyses were computed to test the hypotheses, two for the public organizations and two for the private, considering job satisfaction and affective well-being, respectively, as outcome variables. To prevent problems of multicollineality, these analyses were conducted with centred variables (Aiken & West, 1991), and differential insertion in the hierarchical regression model. In the hierarchical regression analyses, the control variable of gender was introduced in the first step, task conflict, relationship conflict, and culture orientations—support, innovation, goals, and rules—were entered in the second step, and finally, task conflict, relationship conflict interactions, and culture orientation interactions were entered in the third step.

TABLE 1
Number of items, means, standard deviations, and Cronbach's alpha of behavioural variables presented in this study

Variables	α	Public organizations		Private organizations		1	2	3	4	5	6	7	8
		Mean	SD	Mean	SD								
1. Task conflict	.88	2.99	0.92	2.75	0.93	—	.52**	−.23**	−.10	−.22**	−.13*	−.34**	−.22**
2. Relationship conflict	.80	2.84	1.17	2.36	1.04	.34**	—	−.47**	−.22**	−.36**	−.22**	−.50**	−.37**
3. Support	.77	3.27	0.91	3.40	0.85	−.13	−.35**	—	.61**	.54**	.58**	.59**	.29**
4. Innovation	.72	2.70	0.57	3.39	0.66	.06	−.19*	.63**	—	.42**	.65**	.35**	.14*
5. Goals	.81	2.75	0.75	3.40	0.73	−.09	−.37**	.57**	.59**	—	.55**	.43**	.27**
6. Rules	.54	3.55	0.74	3.79	0.83	.09	−.21*	.56**	.69**	.57**	—	.33**	.16*
7. Job satisfaction	.92	4.15	1.13	4.32	1.10	−.29**	−.46**	.59**	.50**	.50**	.45**	—	.45**
8. Well-being	.92	3.86	0.77	3.90	0.82	−.26**	−.45**	.44**	.35**	.37**	.21*	.65**	—

α = Cronbach's alpha coefficient; SD = standard deviation; N public organizations = 360; N private organizations = 169. Correlations above the diagonal belong to public organizations; below the diagonal belong to private organizations.

As can be seen in Table 2, relationship conflict appears to decrease workers' satisfaction and affective well-being, which confirms Hypothesis 1. In contrast, support orientation increases workers' affective well-being and satisfaction. As Hypothesis 2 predicted, there is a significant interaction between task conflict and goal orientation, so that goal orientation moderates the effects of task conflict on satisfaction and affective well-being of private organization employees. Figures 1 and 2 illustrate how

TABLE 2

Regression coefficients between conflict types, culture, satisfaction, and well-being in private organizations

	Satisfaction			Well-being		
Step	R^2	ΔR^2	β	R^2	ΔR^2	β
1. Gender	.01	.01	.15*	.02	.02	.14
2. TC	.51	.49**	−.23**	.30	.28**	−.18*
RC			−.17*			−.21**
Goals			.13			−.15
Rules			.15			.12
Innovation			.11			.14
Support			.24*			.22*
3. TC × RC	.53	.02	−.08	.35	.04	−.17
TC × G			.26*			.37*
TC × R			−.13			−.21
TC × I			−.14			−.19
TC × S			.01			−.01

*$p < .01$; **$p < .001$.   TC: task conflict; RC: relationship conflict; S: support orientation; I: innovation orientation; G: goals orientation; and R: rules orientation.

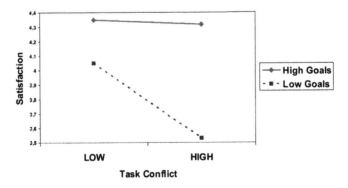

Figure 1. Interaction between task conflict and goal orientation with satisfaction in private organizations.

satisfaction and well-being decrease when task conflict is combined with a low level of goal orientation in organizations.

In the hierarchical regression analyses performed in public organizations gender was entered first, followed in second place by types of conflict and culture orientations—support, innovation, goals, and rules, and third, task conflict and culture orientation interactions. Results are shown in Table 3.

Table 3 provides information about the negative relation between relationship conflict and public organizational workers' satisfaction and

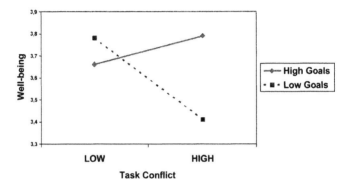

Figure 2. Interaction between task conflict and goal orientation with well-being in private

TABLE 3
Regression coefficients between conflict types, culture, satisfaction, and well-being in public organizations

Step	Satisfaction			Well-being		
	R^2	ΔR^2	β	R^2	ΔR^2	β
1. Gender	.002	.002	.06	.00	.00	− .01
2. TC	.43	.43**	− .10	.16	.16**	.01
RC			− .15*			− .29**
Goals			− .02			− .01
Rules			.11			.07
Innovation			− .05			.04
Support			.46*			.09
3. TC × RC	.46	.03*	.10*	.16	.00	.02
TC × G			.03			.05
TC × R			− .01			− .03
TC × I			− .12			− .12
TC × S			.23**			.09

*$p < .01$; **$p < .001$. TC: task conflict; RC: relationship conflict; S: support orientation; I: innovation orientation; G: goals orientation; and R: rules orientation.

well-being, which confirms Hypothesis 3. In the same way, support orientation is positively related with workers satisfaction. As Hypothesis 4 suggested, there is a significant interaction between task conflict and support orientation with job satisfaction, partially confirming this hypothesis. Figure 3 shows that worker satisfaction decreases when task conflict is combined with a low support orientation in public organizations. There is also a significant interaction between types of conflict—task and relationship conflict—and job satisfaction (Figure 4). Results suggest that when low task conflict is related with low relationship conflict, workers' satisfaction increases.

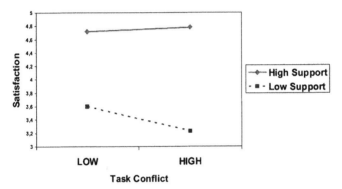

Figure 3.   Interaction between task conflict and support orientation with satisfaction in public organizations.

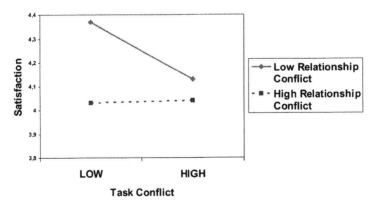

Figure 4.   Interaction between task and relationship conflict with satisfaction in public organizations.

DISCUSSION

The goal of the present study was to analyse the effects of conflict types on the affective reactions of employees and the moderating role that organizational culture plays in this relationship. We analysed two potentially different cultural contexts, that of private organizations and public organizations. The main findings show, first of all, that relationship conflict is negatively related to satisfaction and well-being of members of both public organizations and private organizations. Secondly, the findings show that organizational culture moderates the relationship between task conflict and members' satisfaction and well-being. In this section we discuss the implications of these findings, and examine some strengths and weaknesses of the study design.

As envisaged, relationship conflict hampers satisfaction and well-being of employees of both public and private organizations. In other words, when the members of a working group have incompatible values, beliefs, and ideas, personal tension emerges, and workers' levels of satisfaction and well-being decrease. This result is consistent with previous findings (e.g., De Dreu & Van Vianen, 2001; Surra & Longstreeth, 1990). As Kurtz and Clow (1998) suggest, these affective reactions of employees have important consequences for organizational dynamics, because unsatisfied employees cost companies more than the wages they are paid (Kurtz & Clow, 1998, p. 173). The main reason for the significant impact of human aspects in service organizations is that employees are the basic link between organization and customer, and these employees are often the only ones with whom the client interacts. On the other hand, the study of organizational culture suggests that relationship conflict has a negative impact on daily working practices. This is because employees who perceive a high relationship conflict have a negative perception of the organization and of the activities being performed within it.

Our study also confirmed that under certain circumstances, the consequences of task conflict could be as negative as those of relationship conflict. Our results showed that in private, profit-seeking organizations, task conflict has a negative relationship with workers' satisfaction and well-being. Despite several studies indicating the positive effects of task conflict for these types of organizations (e.g., Jehn et al., 1999; Rollinson, 2002), this study agrees with De Dreu and Weingart's (2003b) meta-analysis, in that disagreements between team members over how to perform a task may interfere with the affective development of its members. When conflicts within the group persist, despite achieving or improving working objectives, the satisfaction and well-being of subjects may be harmed (Jehn, 1995; Ross, 1985).

Task conflict does not have a negative influence on the affective reactions of workers in public organizations. One possible explanation for this evidence may be that workers are more used to conflict at work, due mainly to the decision-making processes of these organizations. As we saw previously, public organizations perceive a higher level of conflict in their working groups. This may be because decisions are taken following extensive discussions between workers, where reaching a consensus is usually the objective. On this point, Falk (1979) demonstrated in an experimental study that democratic decision-making procedures have the potential to facilitate the emergence of task conflict. Another possibility is that workers from public organizations have a high level of job security, so that conflicts are not seen as factors that might jeopardize their jobs. In contrast, in private organizations with much less job security or where employment is of a seasonal nature, workers may see conflicts as job threatening.

Finally, this study confirms that culture moderates the effects of task conflict on workers' affective reactions. One particularly interesting finding suggests that this modulating relationship depends on the type of organization that is analysed. It appears that in private organizations, task conflict is damaging to workers' well-being and satisfaction when there is a low goal orientation within the organization. However, in public organizations task conflict negatively affects satisfaction when there is a low support orientation within the organization. Thus different culture dimensions moderate the relationship between task conflict and workers' affective reactions when private or public organizations are examined.

In private, profit-seeking organizations task conflict does not negatively affect workers' satisfaction and well-being when it is combined with high goal orientation, when performance indicators and achieving goals are important for the team. In this sense, the suggestions that team members might make about procedures for implementing a specific program, or discussions about ways of performing a given task, can have beneficial effects for the team as it develops their ability to adapt to a complex environment and facilitates the understanding of the subjects on which the discussion is based. In short, it encourages constructive debate (Amason, 1996; Jehn et al., 1999) where subjects have the chance to air different points of view, helping to make members feel that they are being listened to and that the decision-making process at work is fair and open. We can conclude, therefore, that task conflict does not negatively influence workers' satisfaction and well-being as long as it occurs in an occupational culture that gives priority to group objectives and in which it is accepted that reward distribution should be guided by the extent to which these objectives are obtained.

In the case of public organizations, our study shows that task conflict does not have negative effects on worker satisfaction when this is combined with high support orientation in work teams; in other words, when the relationship between members of the organization are based on collaboration and mutual assistance, and when group members have high levels of trust and participate and collaborate with their peers in work tasks. This result suggests that to avoid the possible negative effects of task conflict in organizations with a professional bureaucratic structure, where collaboration between workers is vital for obtaining a good level of effectiveness, the conflict needs to occur in a context with high support orientation. Thus, as Jehn and Shah (1997) indicate, the existence of friendship between group members seems to be related both to an improvement in communication channels that influences the creative resolution of conflicts and to an increase in team members' commitment. As a result, the existence of support orientation could prevent task conflict from turning into relationship conflicts (Simons & Peterson, 2000).

Another interesting finding emerging from public organizations is the interaction of both types of conflict with worker satisfaction. The most satisfied workers are those who perceive least conflict—both task and organizational—in their organizations. An explanation for this may lie in the cultural characteristics of public organizations, which are guided more by harmony than conflict and competitiveness.

Some dimensions that differ from public and private organizations could influence in our results. Firstly, public employees enjoy greater job security, because the strength of unions in the regulation of labour relations and the existence of procedures of collective negotiation. The job security climate in public organizations and the important role of unions handling organizational conflicts can explain why task conflict is less negative in these organizations. Secondly, there is less turnovers in public than in private organizations, since temporary contracts are lower in the former—tourism is a seasonal activity in hotels. In public organizations, people have the same colleagues for many years; this might explain why support culture is so relevant. Finally, differences in task—these are less routine in private organizations due to the high variety of customers' needs—can explain the role of task conflict in our results.

The moderating effect of culture on the consequences of task conflict found in this article opens an interesting line for future research. Studies carried out in recent years on this subject have been discouraging, leading many authors to conclude that task conflict may be as negative as relationship conflict (De Dreu & Weingart, 2003b). However, most research into the effects of conflict types, starting with the initial research by Karen Jehn in 1994, has been conducted with management or project teams in which tasks are usually highly creative, with very little standardization and in private organizations with a profit-seeking social role. These previous studies concluded that the stimulation of conflict, both task and relation-ship, may be negative for group performance. The conclusions from this study allows us to consider that conflict may be positive, or at least not negative, when it is activated in certain situations, and in which the team culture has shown itself to be an important variable. It would be interesting to venture deeper into this line of research in the future, considering objective indicators of group performance. Recent research concerning conflict types has tended to use private organizations based on the achievement of goals or objectives, which are known by the workers, and where discussion is encouraged as a way of obtaining these objectives (e.g., Jehn, 1995; Pelled, Eisenhardt, & Xin, 1999). The results from this study illustrate the need to find out more about the implications that differences in organizational culture may have on the effects of intragroup conflict. From this new perspective, it would be interesting to conduct studies contemplating the use of different types of organization.

Some practical implications from the present study concern the improvement of conflict management in the organizational setting. First, before planning an intervention in which task conflict will be activated or encouraged, one needs to understand the type of culture existing in the occupational context that has been chosen. Second, in the private sphere, managers may stimulate already existing discussions about task-related aspects as long as this occurs in a cultural orientation based on the achievement of group objectives. Third, in public organizations, managers may encourage open discussions about task-related aspects as long as they occur in a culture oriented towards the improvement of personal relations and mutual support among its members.

Several limitations of this study should be noted. First, we obtained self-reported measurements of members' perceptions, and, as a consequence, there is a possibility of common method variance. However, this risk is reduced by using standardized instruments (Spector, 1987) as the present study did. The second limitation concerns the use of a cross-sectional design, which did not allow us to check the stability of these apparently positive results over time. Finally, we should point out that the use of a correlational methodology does not guarantee the existence of causal links between them. It would therefore be of interest to perform experimental studies to analyse whether these results are upheld.

Taken together, this study is among the few to demonstrate negative relations between relationship conflict and task conflict. More importantly, this study is the first to show that the type of organization involved and the dominant culture orientation within the organization moderates the negative relationship between task conflict and workers' affective reactions. In private organizations, high goal orientation mitigates the negative effects task conflict can have. In public organizations, it is high levels of support orientation that does the trick.

REFERENCES

Aiken, L. S., & West, S. G. (1991). *Multiple regression: Testing and interpreting interactions.* Newbury Park, CA: Sage.

Amason, A. C. (1996). Distinguishing the effect of functional and dysfunctional conflict on strategic decision making: Resolving a paradox for top management teams. *Academy of Management Journal, 39*, 123–148.

Amason, A. C., & Schweiger, D. M. (1994). Resolving the paradox of conflict, strategic decision making, and organizational performance. *International Journal of Conflict Management, 5*, 239–253.

Baron, R. M. (1991). Positive effects of conflict: A cognitive perspective. *Employee Responsibilities and Rights Journal, 2*, 25–36.

Bourgeois, L. J. (1985). Strategic goals, environmental uncertainty, and economic performance in volatile environments. *Academy of Management Journal, 28*, 548–573.

Cox, K. B. (1998). *Antecedents and effects of intergroup conflict in the nursing unit*. Unpublished doctoral dissertation, Virginia Commonwealth University, Richmond, VA, USA.

De Dreu, C. K. W., Harinck, S., & Van Vianen, A. E. M. (1999). Conflict and performance in groups and organizations. In C. L. Cooper & I. T. Robertson (Eds.), *International review of industrial and organizational psychology*. Chichester, UK: Wiley.

De Dreu, C. K. W., & Van Vianen, A. E. M. (2001). Managing relationship conflict and the effectiveness of organizational teams. *Journal of Organizational Behavior, 22*, 309–328

De Dreu, C. K.W., & Weingart, L. R (2003a). A contingency theory of task conflict and performance in groups and organizational teams. In M. A. West, D. Tjosvold, & K. G. Smith (Eds.), *International handbook of organizational temwork and cooperative working* (pp. 151–166). Chichester, UK: Wiley.

De Dreu, C. K. W., & Weingart, L. R. (2003b). Task versus relationship conflict: A meta-analysis. *Journal of Applied Psychology, 88*, 741–749.

Denhardt, R. B. (1984). *Theories of public organization*. Pacific Grove, CA: Brooks/Cole.

Eisenhardt, K., & Schoonhoven, C. (1990). Organizational growth: Linking founding team, strategy, environment, and growth among U.S. semiconductor ventures, 1978–1988. *Administrative Science Quarterly, 35*, 504–529.

Falk, G. (1979). When does majority role facilitate task conflict in problem solving groups? *Academy of Management Proceedings*, 326–330.

Friedman, R. A., Tidd, S. T., Currall, S. C., & Tsai, J. C. (2000). What goes around comes around: The impact of personal conflict style on work conflict and stress. *International Journal of Conflict Management, 11*, 32–55.

Guetzkow, H., & Gyr, J. (1954). An analysis of conflict in decision-making groups. *Human Relations, 7*, 367–381.

Hooijberg, R., & Choi, J. (2001). The impact of organizational characteristics on leadership effectiveness models: An examination of leadership in a private and a public sector organization. *Administration and Society, 33*, 403–431.

Jehn, K. A. (1994). Enhancing effectiveness: An investigation of advantages and disadvantages of value-based intragroup conflict. *International Journal of Conflict Management, 5*, 223–238.

Jehn, K. A. (1995). A multimethod examination of the benefits and detriments of intragroup conflict. *Administrative Science Quarterly, 40*, 256–282.

Jehn, K. A. (1997). A qualitative analysis of conflict types and dimensions in organizational groups. *Administrative Science Quarterly, 42*, 530–557.

Jehn, K. A., Chadwick, C., & Thatcher, S. M. B. (1997). To agree or not agree: The effects of value congruence, individual demographic dissimilarity, and conflict on workgroup outcomes. *International Journal of Conflict Management, 8*, 287–305.

Jehn, K. A., Northcraft, G. B., & Neale, M. A. (1999). Why differences make a difference: A field study of diversity, conflict, and performance in workgroups. *Administrative Science Quarterly, 44*, 741–763.

Jehn, K. A., & Shah, P. (1997). Interpersonal relationship and task performance: An examination of mediating processes in friendship and acquaintance groups. *Journal of Personality and Social Psychology, 72,* 775–790.

Kabanoff, B. (1991). Equity, equality, power and conflict. *Academy of Management Review, 16,* 416–441.

Korsgaard, M. A., Schweiger, D. M., & Sapienza, H. J. (1995). Building commitment, attachment, and trust in top management teams: The role of procedural justice. *Academy of Management Journal, 38,* 60–84.

Kurtz, D. L., & Clow, K. E. (1998). *Services marketing.* New York: John Wiley & Sons.

Mañas, M. A., González-Romá, V., & Peiró, J. M. (1999). *El clima de los equipos de trabajo: determinantes y consecuencias* [Climate in work groups: Predictors and consequences]. Almería, Spain: Universidad de Almería, Servicio de Publicaciones, Instituto de Estudios Almerienses.

Meliá, J. L., & Peiró, J. M. (1989). La medida de la satisfacción laboral en contextos organizacionales: el cuestionario de satisfacción S20/23 [A measure of satisfaction in organizational settings: The S20/23 satisfaction questionnaire]. *Psicologemas, 3,* 59–74.

Mintzberg, H. (1979). *The structuring of organizations: A synthesis of the research.* Englewood Cliffs, NJ: Prentice Hall.

Murnighan, J. K., & Conlon, D. E. (1991). The dynamics of intense work groups: A study of British string quartets. *Administrative Science Quarterly, 36,* 165–186.

Nemeth, C. (1986). Differential contributions of majority and minority influence. *Psychological Review, 93,* 23–32.

Pelled, L. H., Eisenhardt, K. M., & Xin, K. R. (1999). Exploring the black box: An analysis of work group diversity, conflict, and performance. *Administrative Science Quarterly, 44,* 1–28.

Perry, J., & Rainey, H. (1988). The public–private distinction in organization theory: A critique and research strategy. *Academy of Management Review, 13,* 182–201.

Pinkley, R. L. (1990). Dimensions of conflict frame: Disputant interpretations of conflict. *Journal of Applied Psychology, 75,* 117–126.

Pondy, L. R. (1967). Organizational conflict: Concepts and models. *Administrative Science Quarterly, 12,* 296–320.

Porter, L. W., Lawler, E. E., & Hackman, J. R. (1975). *Behavior in organizations.* New York: McGraw-Hill.

Quinn, R. E. (1988). *Beyond rational management.* San Francisco: Jossey-Bass.

Ring, P. S., & Perry, J. L. (1985). Strategic management in public and private organizations: Implications of distinctive contexts and constraints. *Academy of Management Review, 10,* 276–286.

Robertson, P. J., & Seneviratne, S. J. (1995). Outcomes of planned organizational change in the public sector: A meta-analytic comparison to the private sector. *Public Administration Review, 55,* 547–558.

Rollinson, D. (2002). *Organizational behavior.* Boston: Addison-Wesley.

Ross, R. S. (1985). Issues of level in organizational research. In L. L. Cummings & B. M. Staw (Eds.), *Research in organizational behavior* (Vol. 7, pp. 1–37). Greenwich, CT: JAI Press.

Simons, T. L., & Peterson, R. S. (2000). Task conflict and relationship conflict in top management teams: The pivotal role of intragroup trust. *Journal of Applied Psychology, 85,* 102–111.

Spector, P. E. (1987). Method variance as an artefact in self-reported affect and perceptions at work: Myth or significant problems. *Journal of Applied Psychology, 72,* 438–443.

Spector, P. E., & Jex, S. M. (1998). Development of tour self-report measures of job stressors and strain: Interpersonal conflict at work scale, organizational constraints scale, quantitative workload inventory, and physical symptoms inventory. *Journal of Occupational Health Psychology, 3,* 356–367.

Surra, C., & Longstreeth, M. (1990). Similarity of outcomes, interdependence and conflict in dating relationships. *Journal of Personality and Social Psychology, 59*, 501–516.

Thomas, K. W. (1992). Conflict and negotiation processes in organizations. In M. D. Dunnette & L. M. Hough (Eds.), *Handbook of industrial and organizational psychology* (2nd ed., pp. 651–717). Palo Alto, CA: Consulting Psychologist Press.

Tjosvold, D., Dann, V., & Wong, C. (1992). Managing conflict between departments to serve customers. *Human Relations, 45*, 1035–1054.

Van de Vliert, E., & de Dreu, C. K. W. (1994). Optimizing performance by conflict stimulation. *International Journal of Conflict Management, 5*, 211–222.

Van Muijen, J. J., & Koopman, P. L. (1994). The influence of national culture on organizational culture: A comparative study between 10 countries. *The European Work and Organizational Psychologist, 4*, 367–380.

Van Muijen, J. J., Koopman, P. L., Dondeyne, P., De Cock, G., & De Witte, K. (1992). Organizational culture, the development of an international instrument for comparing countries. In G. Hunyady (Ed.), *Proceedings of the second European congress of psychology* (pp. 249–259). Budapest, Hungary: A jtósi Dúver.

Van Muijen, J., et al. (1999). Organizational culture: The Focus Questionnaire. *European Journal of Work and Organizational Psychology, 8*, 551–568.

Warr, P. (1990). The measurement of wellbeing and other aspects of mental health. *Journal of Occupational Psychology, 63*, 193–210.

West, M. A., & Anderson, N. R. (1996). Innovation in top management teams. *Journal of Applied Psychology, 81*, 680–693.

West, M. A., & Wallace, M. (1991). Innovation in health care teams. *European Journal of Social Psychology, 21*, 303–315.

EUROPEAN JOURNAL OF WORK AND
ORGANIZATIONAL PSYCHOLOGY
2005, 14 (2), 177–203

Intergroup conflict and intergroup effectiveness in organizations: Theory and scale development

Andreas W. Richter, Judy Scully, and Michael A. West

Aston Business School, Aston University, Birmingham, UK

Many see the absence of conflict between groups as indicative of effective intergroup relations. Others consider its management a suitable effectiveness criterion. In this article we demarcate a different approach and propose that these views are deficient in describing effective intergroup relations. The article theorizes alternative criteria of intergroup effectiveness rooted in team representatives' subjective value judgements and assesses the psychometric characteristics of a short measure based on these criteria. Results on empirical validity suggest the measure to be a potential alternative outcome of organizational conflict. Implications for both the study of intergroup relations and conflict theory are discussed.

With increasing complexity and environmental demands, organizations specialize and diversify their workforce, adopting team-based structures, in order to bundle and focus efforts to most efficiently handle their subtasks (Lawrence & Lorsch, 1967b; McCann & Galbraith, 1981). The completion of subtasks is, however, only useful when organizations manage to coordinate and integrate these "parts" into a "whole". Utilizing these combined resources can be a challenge for team-based organizations, due to structural and psychological barriers between groups that hinder effective intergroup relations (Lawrence & Lorsch, 1967b; Van Knippenberg, 2003; see also Alderfer, 1986): Groups pursue their own interests at the expense of the overall organizational goal (Tjosvold, 1991); they compete over scarce resources (Mohrmann, Cohen, & Mohrmann, 1995); and fail to manage the disruptive dynamics of social categorization (Terry & Callan, 1998). Dutton and Walton (1966) describe how manufacturing units' preference for long, economic runs conflicts with sales units' preference for quick delivery to good

Correspondence should be addressed to Andreas Richter, Work and Organizational Psychology Group, Aston Business School, University of Aston, Birmingham B4 7ET, UK. Email: richteaw@aston.ac.uk

This research was enabled through a grant to the first author by the German Academic Exchange Service (DAAD). We are grateful to Jeremy Dawson for advice on statistical issues.

http://www.tandf.co.uk/journals/pp/1359432X.html   DOI: 10.1080/13594320444000263

customers. Such conflicts of interest are frequently fostered by management rewarding group effectiveness at the expense of the development and maintenance of effective lateral relationships (see Hartley, 1996). But is there a difference between conflict-free and effective intergroup relations, and if so, how is organizational conflict related to intergroup effectiveness?

To answer this question we need a measure other than intergroup conflict to assess the quality and effectiveness of how dyads or sets of groups perform their collaborative tasks. In order to develop such a measure, we first need to clarify what exactly characterizes well-developed, effective relationships between groups.

In the following section we review existing approaches to intergroup effectiveness. We conclude this review by proposing four criteria that characterize the effectiveness of lateral relationships. These criteria are based on team representatives' value judgements and represent potential alternative outcomes of organizational conflict. In the remainder of the article we examine the psychometric properties of a scale measuring these criteria.

WHAT IS INTERGROUP EFFECTIVENESS?

Existing conceptualizations of effective intergroup relations

Defining key concepts. Our search for intergroup effectiveness criteria was guided by our definitions of group, intergroup relations, intergroup transactions, and intergroup effectiveness. We define an organizational group as a set of individuals who perceive themselves and whom nonmembers perceive as constituting an identifiable social aggregate within the organization (Brett & Rognes, 1986). The terms team and group are used interchangeably, for the academic literature prefers the term group, but groups in organizations are frequently referred to as teams. We define intergroup relations as activities that occur between and/or among groups (Alderfer, 1986, p. 190). An intergroup transaction occurs "whenever individuals belonging to one group interact collectively or individually with another group or its members in terms of their group identifications" (Sherif, 1966, p. 9). Thus, intergroup transactions may occur between group representatives who represent their groups' interests, not their own, on behalf of their group. Intergroup effectiveness is then the product of an intergroup transaction and consequently a concept that needs to be conceptually allocated at the intergroup level.

We will revert to two separate lines of literature deemed most fruitful in our search for candidates of effective intergroup relations: As intergroup effectiveness represents a layer of organizational effectiveness, we refer to the organizational effectiveness literature. Secondly, we review this body of the organizational intergroup relations literature that is most concerned with the exchange and output of dyads or sets of groups, the dispute resolution literature.

The organizational effectiveness literature. The empirical and theoretical literature on organizational effectiveness generally distinguishes three levels: Individual, group, and organizational effectiveness (Jones, 1997). The classical models of group effectiveness subsume groups' relationships with other groups within the "input" or "context" category that impact on group processes and group effectiveness (e.g., Hackman, 1987). These models are therefore not suitable for capturing how interdependent groups operate as a functional synergistic entity, as a larger work unit (Mathieu, Marks, & Zaccaro, 2001). Others, mostly adopting an open system perspective, rather stress groups' active role in shaping and managing their environment, thereby more actively integrating group members' external strategies and boundary management into their models of group effectiveness (e.g., Gladstein, 1984). However, these models do not actually explicate how dyads or sets of groups co- and interact in pursuit of common goals either. Conceptually, as with other group effectiveness models, single group effectiveness is the only outcome variable.

Mathieu and colleagues (Mathieu et al., 2001) present a theoretical framework of Multi Team Systems (MTSs) that demarcates the effectiveness with which dyads or sets of groups perform collaborative tasks. An MTS is defined as a functional collective network of two or more teams operating within or across organizational boundaries. It describes a "team of teams", a functional collective, which forms a network operating in an environment that demands both coordinated interteam and intrateam behaviours in order to succeed. MTS boundaries are defined by virtue of the fact that all teams within the system, while pursuing different proximal goals, share at least one common distal goal, and therefore exhibit interdependence with at least one other team in the system. No one individual team can single-handedly accomplish an MTS superordinate goal. Mathieu and colleagues illustrate this by describing how fire-fighter and ambulance teams have to closely synchronize their efforts in order to quickly and safely extract injured motorists from the crash scenes. Effectiveness of an MTS is therefore defined not only in terms of how well each team accomplishes its proximal goals, but more importantly on how well different teams collectively accomplish shared goals at higher levels of the goal hierarchy.

Dispute resolution literature. In contrast to the organizational effectiveness literature, the dispute resolution literature suggests the successful management of intergroup conflict or conflict-free relationships, respectively, to be suitable candidates for effective intergroup relations.

Walton's theory of lateral relationships (1966) provides a description of effective intergroup relations in terms of intergroup behaviour, intergroup attitudes, and the formation of the intergroup structure. The theory distinguishes integrative (effective) from distributive (ineffective) intergroup relations. Integrative intergroup relations are characterized by a problem-solving decision-making mode; positive attitudes, namely trust, friendliness, and the inclusion of the other unit; and interaction patterns that are flexible, informal, and open. Conversely, distributive intergroup relations are characterized by a bargaining decision-making mode of careful rationing and deliberate distortion of information; rigid, negative attitudes like suspicion, hostility, and dissociation from the other unit; and a formal and circumscribed structure of interaction.

Among Walton's factors, bargaining and problem-solving decision making in particular has attracted the attention of many researchers investigating effective intergroup relations. In short, a problem-solving approach is considered most constructive as it aims for a settlement that integrates the goals of both parties (Blake, Sheppard, & Mouton, 1966; De Dreu, Harinck, & Van Vianen, 1999; Lawrence & Lorsch, 1967a; Nauta & Sanders, 2000; Thomas, 1992). For example, Lawrence and Lorsch (1967a) compared six plastic firms and found that interunit cooperation was more effectively achieved to the extent that managers openly confronted differences rather than smoothed them over or forced decisions. However, in contrast to Walton's framework, the literature tends to consider negotiation style as a means by which to resolve or manage conflict, rather than an effectiveness criterion by itself (e.g., Blake et al., 1966; Lawrence & Lorsch, 1967b; Nauta & Sanders, 2000). The endurance of the negotiated settlement of the conflict resolution and participants' evaluation of processes and outcomes in terms of procedural and distributive justice are cited as additional important criteria for effective intergroup relations (Brett & Rognes, 1986).

Social Identity Theory (SIT; Tajfel, 1978; Tajfel & Turner, 1979; see also Haslam, 2001) may represent the dominant paradigm in investigating relationships among organizational groups. SIT proposes that a potentially important and positively valued component of people's identities derives from their group memberships, and that these positively valued "social identities" are maintained primarily by means of social comparison processes of ingroup members with relevant outgroups (Festinger, 1954). According to SIT, group members may develop conflicting relationships with outgroup members, in order to enhance their positively valued social identities. Considering the disruptive dynamics of social categorization as the basis for intergroup conflict implies that the successful management of social categorization characterizes effective intergroup relations (cf. Brewer & Brown, 1998; Haslam, 2001). Suggestions of how to accomplish this vary from enhancing organizational identification (Richter, Van Dick, & West, 2004), fostering mere contact (Allport, 1954), to redrawing group boundaries by means of cross-, de-, or re-categorization, respectively (Brewer & Brown, 1998). However, there is growing evidence from social psychological research suggesting that intergroup bias is affected by the interdependence between groups (e.g., Gaertner et al., 1999). Even though social identity dynamics do operate in the absence of any differential interdependence, growing evidence from experimental social psychology suggests that negative interdependence between groups (in the form of noncorrespondence of outcomes) intensifies hostile intergroup behaviour (Schopler et al., 2001; for an overview, see Wildschut, Pinter, Vevea, Insko, & Schopler, 2003).

A different line of intergroup conflict research explicitly shifts the focus from cognitive processes of individuals to such structural characteristics of interdependent organizational groups. Notably the imbalance of both differentiation of subsystems and the need for integrating these subsystems in pursue of superordinate organizational goals represents an inherent potential for interface or structural conflict between work units (Blake et al., 1966; Lawrence & Lorsch, 1967b). Such interface conflict is characterized by groups who find themselves in negative interdependence with the likely result that one group's goal achievement decreases the possibility of another group's goal achievement (cf. Thomas, 1992). Research based on realistic conflict theory (Sheriff, 1966) as well as the theory of competition and cooperation (Deutsch, 1973; Tjosvold, 1998) similarly stress that effective intergroup relations are rooted in the cooperative rather than competitive interdependence between groups. In support of this theory, Tjosvold, Dann, and Wong (1992) found that under conditions of cooperative interdependence representatives from divergent departments approached problems that emerged at the interface between groups in an open-minded manner. Such constructive controversy was then positively related to the extent to which customers were well served, to efficiency, and to the extent that group leaders believed they can work with the other productively in the future. Similarly, discussing views openly and cooperatively helped managers of different departments to win engineering contracts and improve productivity in a large consultancy firm (Tjosvold, 1988). These studies suggest that perceptions of positive interdependence between groups represent the basis for effective intergroup relations.

Brett and Rognes (1986) further developed Williamson's (1975) concept of transaction costs for their criteria of intergroup effectiveness. This refers to the costs that emerge from the interaction of two groups when at least one of the parties pursues its own interests rather than maximizing the two parties' joint benefits. Transaction costs can take the two forms that parties either engage in needless haggling over the terms of the transaction, or the terms of the transaction are advantageous to one party but suboptimal for the relationship as a whole.

The authors argue that transaction costs at the intergroup level of conceptualization consist of the two elements quality and efficiency. Either element is a consequence of how intergroup conflict is dealt with. Quality refers to the degree to which the intergroup negotiation results in a well-defined exchange agreement. If the quality is poor, then negotiations will be reopened after a settlement, because settlement was either incomplete or ill defined. Efficiency refers to the costs associated with the establishment of transaction terms, that is human and other resources expended during intergroup negotiations. These costs may emerge in the form of constraints on both intragroup and intergroup activities, as well as human resource costs associated with developing the transaction terms. The authors argue that both quality and efficiency need to be balanced in order to assess the effectiveness of an intergroup relationship. So incurred costs do not necessarily have to be an indicator of reduced effectiveness; high quality interface solutions and enduring agreements between teams may simply require high costs, but pay off in the long run if they endure and are accepted by both parties. Brett and Rognes' conceptualization is doubtlessly a major step in the development of intergroup effectiveness criteria. However, their rationale is based on the two premises that the reason for interaction between groups is to exchange resources, and that criteria are based on the transformation of a conflict into action by both groups.

Evaluation of the dispute resolution and organizational effectiveness literature. In many of the outlined conceptualizations of effective intergroup relations, three aspects appear critical.

Firstly, most approaches are based on the assumption that conflict between groups is both frequent and dysfunctional. Consequently, the absence of conflict, the transformation of a dispute into action, or the well-negotiated outcome are features of effective intergroup relations. This assumption seems obvious as the potential for intergroup conflict is inherent in team-based organizations due to both structural characteristics and social categorization processes (see Hartley, 1996; Van Knippenberg, 2003). Nevertheless, even though relationships between groups may bear considerable conflict potential (Thomas, 1992), they do not necessarily have to be rich in conflicts, or may be conflictory in some aspects, but harmonious in others. Several authors report case studies of harmonious relationships between groups as characterized by a friendly, cohesive intergroup atmosphere (Blake et al., 1966; Lawrence & Lorsch, 1967b), even under conditions of considerable conflict potential, as it exists between production and sales departments (Dutton & Walton, 1966). Conversely, intergroup conflict does not have to be detrimental for organizations (Putnam, 1997); little or no conflict may even result in stagnation, poor decisions, and ineffectiveness (Rahim, 2001, p. 12), whereas positive effects of intergroup conflict include motivation through competition, enhancement of stability in the system through channelled interunit contact, and rigidity and formality in decision procedures (Dutton & Walton, 1969). Yet, most approaches are built upon the existence of dysfunctional conflict between groups, and are therefore deficient in explaining the effectiveness with which harmonious dyads of groups perform their collective tasks.

Secondly, most approaches (e.g., Brett & Rognes, 1986) are based on the assumption that groups solely interact to exchange valuable resources. This rationale, however, does not take into consideration that groups may also interact as one synergistic entity in order to accomplish the overall organizational goals (Tjosvold, 1991; Van de Ven & Ferry, 1980, p. 300). The integration of differentiated units in order to produce integrative outcomes or services can be crucial for organizational effectiveness (see Mathieu et al., 2001). The second important point being made is that the criteria of intergroup effectiveness should therefore include such collective services or products that are cooperatively generated by different groups.

Finally, we argue that there is a varying understanding of whether effective intergroup relations are best characterized by intergroup attitudes (e.g., trust, bias), intergroup behaviour (i.e., integrative negotiation style), conflict free relationships, aspects of superordinate goal accomplishment, or comprises aspects of each. We proposed earlier that intergroup effectiveness is the *product* of intergroup transactions occurring between boundary spanners (i.e., those group members involved in intergroup transactions) or entire groups. We thus focus on the *output in the form of a product or service* of these transactions. A group dyad may produce such an output, even under conditions of high conflict, dysfunctional attitudes, and behaviour. The final important point therefore is that we explicitly demarcate our criteria of intergroup effectiveness from intergroup attitudes, negotiation style, and intergroup conflict.

An integrative framework for criteria of intergroup effectiveness

In response to our criticism, we began the development of meaningful criteria of intergroup effectiveness with the question of why different groups interact. Such a perspective may allow us both to avoid criterion deficiency and to integrate existing conceptualizations. Additionally, it may divert attention away from the transformation of conflict as the basis of effective intergroup relations. Van de Ven and Ferry (1980) distinguished two causes for the development and maintenance of intergroup relationships.

The resource dependence model is consistent with former approaches (e.g., Brett & Rognes, 1986; cf. Aiken & Hage, 1968) and argues that groups interact with other groups because of their need for resources. Therefore, the causation of the relationship, the need for valuable resources, lies *within* the groups. Consequently, the extent of resource provision and utilization between groups is an important criterion of intergroup effectiveness.

Complementary to this model is the organizational system position. This perspective argues that different groups also interact in order to respond to system problems, emerging opportunities, or mandates within the groups' organizational environment. According to this perspective, the causation of the intergroup relationship lies within the groups' environment and therefore *outside* the group. Both positions are in line with Mathieu and colleagues (Mathieu et al., 2001) as well as Tjosvold's (1998) rationale as they are related to the attainment of or rate of progress towards the achievement of superordinate goals. The extent to which both teams effectively respond to their environment would thus represent a second criterion.

Regardless of the cause of cross-group working, we propose two additional criteria most relevant for effective collaboration between groups.

The first is the concept of transaction costs in the form of Brett and Rognes' (1986) efficiency and quality criterion. Ineffective intergroup relations are characterized by unreasonably high transaction costs, as indicated by a high ratio of invested resources to the quality of the outcome.

The final criterion refers to the viability of the intergroup relationship. If both groups do not honour their responsibilities and commitments towards each other and perceive the give and take relationship between both parties as unfair, resource exchange and efficient coordination may be reduced. Such unreliable or unbalanced relationships may lead to groups working in isolation or building alternative relationships with other work units.

Despites the theoretical utility of distinguishing different reasons why groups interact, groups may most likely cooperate in order to both provide each other with valuable resources and to work on collaborative mandates, problems, or opportunities; similarly, complex tasks may embrace aspects of both. From there, it is proposed that the subfactors yield one superordinate factor of intergroup effectiveness, as illustrated by Figure 1.

From this analysis we set about developing a measure of intergroup effectiveness and the methods employed are described below.

METHOD

Item generation

The aim was to create a parsimonious and short measure of intergroup effectiveness that could easily be administered within a larger survey. An initial item pool of 24 items capturing the four theoretical criteria (6 items per category) was compiled by the first author. Since the goals a dyad

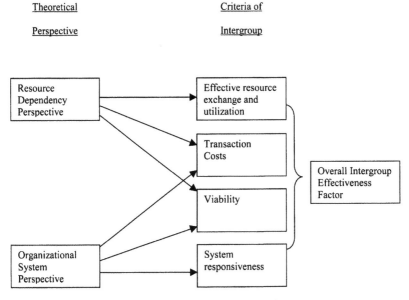

Figure 1. Criteria of intergroup effectiveness.

follows may not result in the dyad's objective output but rather be based on boundary spanners' subjective attitudes and perceptions, items reflected value judgements of the boundary spanners' subjective believes and attitudes (see Van de Ven & Ferry, 1980, p. 417). Following Brett and Rognes (1986), items meant to represent the product of an intergroup interaction; to characterize the relationship over time; and to represent an index of the quality of the relationship. As items were conceptualized at the intergroup level, item wording matched this level using an intergroup referent (e.g., "To what extent did *both teams work effectively together* in order to provide better services to patients?") (cf. Klein, Conn, Smith, & Sorra, 2001). Since some items with an intergroup referent appeared difficult to understand, these items were worded in such a way that two separate items assessed the perspective of each group of the dyad (e.g., "For *this other team* to accomplish its goals and responsibilities, to what extent did it receive the expected services, resources, or support from *your team*?" in addition to "For *your team* to accomplish its goals and responsibilities, to what extent did you receive the expected services, resources, or support from *this other team*?"). The pool also included five items from an existing measure of intergroup effectiveness (Van de Ven & Ferry, 1980).

Three subject matter experts (PhD students familiar with research on teams and intergroup relations) were then asked to assign the items blindly to one of the four criteria in order to confirm the four-partite factor structure. Additionally, they were asked to indicate how difficult they found this assignment on a 1 – 5 Likert scale. Items allocated by more than one expert in a deviant category or rated as difficult to assign were excluded from further analysis. For those items where one expert disagreed with the others, differences were discussed, and it was assessed whether they were due to either different perceptions of what the items measure or weaknesses in the wording of the items. Either deletion or rewording of items, respectively, terminated the development process. The instrument was then given to six individuals working in three different health care organizations as well as a pilot team of one of the five participating organizations. Comments resulted in slight amendments of the measure. The scale is outlined in the Appendix.

Procedure

Five Primary Care Trusts (PCTs) across the UK agreed to participate in a survey study about intergroup relations. PCTs are team-based health care organizations pertaining to the British National Health Service. As multiple team membership was common in these organizations, the first author identified the "principal teams", where staff were primarily attached to, and invited them to participate. Management teams were excluded in order to avoid power asymmetries between teams at different hierarchical levels. Each team that agreed to participate was asked to agree upon one other team within the organization (apart from management) they worked the closest with. This was done to ensure both interaction frequency and high interdependence between teams. All questions on intergroup relations referred to this other team. The survey was disseminated to 448 individuals of 56 teams, and 230 staff belonging to 54 teams returned surveys, yielding an individual level response rate of 51%. The resulting sample of teams varied across departments, service teams, and administration teams. 194 participants (88%) were female, which is not surprising as a great part of teams were nursing teams. A selection question that asked whether team members did interact on work-related matters with members of the other team allowed to identify 210 individuals as the teams' boundary spanners, those individuals involved with members of the other team. These individuals answered the questions on intergroup effectiveness. Boundary spanners are considered the most suitable assessors of effectiveness, as these individuals are directly involved in intergroup transactions (Van de Ven & Ferry, 1980). As their judgements may, however, be prone to self-serving bias, we also asked teams to consent that the researcher approaches their line manager in order to obtain external ratings of team and interteam effectiveness. 48 teams agreed, and a total of 41 external ratings was obtained. Of those 41 managers, 36 returned ratings five months later at T2.

RESULTS

The remainder of this article is concerned with examining the psychometric properties of the intergroup effectiveness scale. We carried out individual level analysis to examine both construct validity (using confirmatory factor analysis) and discriminant validity (using exploratory factor analysis). We then aggregated the data to the team level. Consensual and discriminable validity was examined in order to justify aggregation. Further support for consensual validity was provided by examining correspondence of perceptions of four pure team dyads, as well as examining correlations of both self- and external ratings. Data on internal homogeneity and predictive validity conclude the analysis.

Individual-level analysis

Construct validity. We tested the model using confirmatory factor analysis (CFA) with AMOS version 3.51 (Arbuckle, 1995). Following the presented rationale, we tested the hypothesized four-factor model (representing the four subfactors of intergroup effectiveness) against a one-factor model (assuming participants do not differentiate between subfactors, but an intergroup effectiveness factor does exist) and a null-factor model (the data does not yield a single factor). The four-factor model was tested with both uncorrelated factors (indicative that no superordinate intergroup effectiveness factor exists) and correlated factors (indicative that a superordinate factor exists). As CFA yielded an initial poor fit for the four- and the one-factor models, we deleted four items based on the suggested modification indices. The resulting 12 items are included in Table 2 (see page 189).

Table 1 illustrates fit indices for the model based on the remaining 12 items. Low χ^2 and RMR values as well as high GFI and TLI values are suggestive of good model fit. In particular, for the TLI and GFI index, recommended levels of fit are above .90. Recommended values for the ratio of χ^2 indices to degrees of freedom (χ^2/df) are below 2, and for the RMR below .10, respectively (cf. Marsh, Balla, & Hau, 1996). χ^2 values are more depending on sample size than others, e.g., the TLI values (Gerbing & Anderson, 1993). Nevertheless, artificially reduced χ^2 values are rather a problem for big sample sizes than for small ones like ours. Only the correlated four-factor model reaches the recommended values for the ratio of χ^2 values to degrees of freedom (χ^2/df) below 2, RMR values below .10, and TLI and GFI values above .90. We tested the improvement of model fit by calculating the differences of χ^2 values in relation to the differences in degrees of freedom ($\Delta\chi^2/\Delta df$) for each model. The test indicates a significant model improvement for the correlated four-factor model over the one-factor

TABLE 1
Fit indices of confirmatory factor analysis for the intergroup effectiveness scale

	χ^2	df	GFI	RMR	χ^2/df	TLI
Null model	1114.49	66	.36	.31	15.49	
Four-factors (uncorrelated) [a]	396.31	56	.74	.24	7.08	.62
One-factor[b]	369.03	54	.72	.11	6.83	.63
Four-factors (correlated)[c]	95.34	48	.92	.05	1.99	.94

$N = 156$; GFI = goodness-of-fit index; TLI = Tucker Lewis index; RMR = root mean square residual.
[a]Difference four-factor (uncorrelated) and null-model: $\Delta\chi^2(df) = 718.18(11)^{***}$.
[b]Difference one-factor and four-factor model (uncorrelated): $\Delta\chi^2(df) = 27.28(2)^{***}$.
[c]Difference four-factor (correlated) and one-factor model (correlated): $\Delta\chi^2(df) = 273.69(6)^{***}$.

model $(\Delta\chi^2/\Delta df) = 273.69(6)$, $p < .001$ (Table 1), suggesting that the correlated four-factor model fits the data best.

Discriminant validity. We then assessed the measure's discriminant validity by carrying out exploratory factor analysis with items measuring *team effectiveness, intergroup conflict, intergroup negotiation style, intergroup attitudes*, and *intergroup effectiveness*. The scales measured team performance standards (Vinokur-Kaplan, 1995), goal conflict between teams (adopted from Tjosvold, 1991), forcing and problem-solving negotiation style (De Dreu, Evers, Beersma, Kluwer, & Nauta, 2001), and intergroup trust (Cummings & Bromiley, 1996) in addition to our intergroup effectiveness items. High discriminant validity would be indicated if the factor structure clearly differentiates intergroup effectiveness from other scales. Additionally, we expected the intergroup effectiveness subscales to load on different factors, thereby providing additional support for the construct's four-factor structure.

Table 2 indicates that differential validity is supported inasmuch as the intergroup effectiveness subscales load on different factors than the other intergroup variables do. The data therefore suggests intergroup effectiveness to be distinct from team effectiveness, intergroup conflict, negotiation style, and intergroup trust. The relationships among the intergroup effectiveness subscales, however, are controversial. Whilst viability and transaction costs are clearly identified as separate factors, system responsiveness and resource exchange load on the same factor. Thus, contrary to our rationale, participants may not distinguish very well between both. One possible explanation for this would be that the tasks the team dyads are working on could involve both the exchange of resources between teams and their response to problems, mandates, or opportunities within the organization. Also, working together on tasks within the broader organization may

TABLE 2
Principal axis factor analysis of self-report data; pattern matrix, oblique rotation

	I Intergroup trust	II Transaction costs	III Team effectiveness	IV Forcing	V Problem solving	VI Intergroup conflict	VII Resource exchange/system responsiveness	VIII Viability	IX
1. The goals of both teams are not reconcilable with each other.	.01	−.00	.09	.01	−.03	.18	.05	−.20	**−.62**
2. Both teams try to show that they are superior to each other.	−.02	.04	−.05	.08	.02	**.77**	−.01	.05	−.08
3. Team members structure things in ways that favour their own goals rather than the goals of the other team.	−.02	.09	−.07	−.17	−.04	**.67**	.10	−.06	.06
4. Both teams have a "win–lose" relationship.	−.09	.07	.05	−.08	.03	**.54**	.07	−.05	−.18
5. Team members give high priority to the things their team wants to accomplish and low priority to the things members of the other team want to accomplish.	−.17	.00	−.02	−.13	−.02	**.46**	.06	−.10	.01
6. I feel that the people in the other team negotiate with us honestly.	**.76**	.00	.10	−.05	.04	−.21	.01	−.02	.03
7. I feel that people in the other team negotiate joint expectations fairly.	**.46**	−.13	.02	−.07	−.13	−.28	.05	.17	−.11
8. I think that the people in the other team meet their negotiated obligations to our team.	**.70**	−.20	.06	−.07	−.04	.00	−.11	.12	−.01
9. In my opinion, people in the other team are reliable.	**.64**	−.01	.01	.02	−.07	−.04	−.28	−.10	.03
10. I examine ideas from both sides to find a mutually optimal solution.	.08	−.10	.06	.18	**−.63**	−.06	.06	−.05	.14

(continued overleaf)

TABLE 2
(continued)

	I Intergroup trust	II Transaction costs	III Team effectiveness	IV Forcing	V Problem solving	VI Intergroup conflict	VII Resource exchange/system respon-siveness	VIII Viability	IX
11. I work out a solution that serves my own as well as the other team's interests as far as possible.	−.02	−.03	.06	−.02	**−.56**	.01	.02	.15	−.06
12. I examine issues until I find a solution that really satisfies me and the other party.	−.04	−.08	−.04	−.02	**−.71**	.07	−.16	.04	−.12
13. I stand up for my own and the other's goals and interests.	−.06	.22	−.07	−.21	**−.49**	−.05	−.04	−.08	.04
14. I do everything to win.	.14	.15	−.00	**−.54**	.01	.01	.00	−.01	−.05
15. I push my own point of view.	−.08	−.09	.02	**.61**	−.11	.07	.08	−.00	.05
16. I search for gains.	−.00	.05	.01	**−.57**	.01	−.05	−.10	.07	−.12
17. I fight for a good outcome for myself.	−.01	−.17	−.02	**−.70**	.04	.08	.00	−.04	.08
18. Our team met the standards of quality expected by the PCT.	.04	−.00	**.79**	.06	−.01	.03	−.02	.09	−.16
19. Our team met the standards of quantity expected by the PCT.	.07	.08	**.72**	.05	−.08	.04	−.03	−.02	.09
20. Our team met the standards of timeliness expected by the PCT.	.01	−.13	**.78**	−.00	.09	.05	.01	.04	.06
21. Our team met the standards of implementation expected by the PCT.	−.02	−.11	**.79**	−.12	.04	−.10	.00	.03	−.00
22. Our team had a reputation for work excellence within the PCT.	−.02	.13	**.73**	−.02	−.05	−.06	−.01	−.05	−.07

TABLE 2
(continued)

	I	II	III	IV	V	VI	VII	VIII	IX
	Intergroup trust	Transaction costs	Team effectiveness	Forcing	Problem solving	Intergroup conflict	Resource exchange/system respon-siveness	Viability	
23. To what extent did working with this other team result in too many constraints (e.g., time/staff shortage, etc.) on your team's everyday activities?	−.05	**.58**	.09	.01	.02	.09	.01	−.07	.16
24. To what extent did working with this other team entail too much lost time and energy spent on trying to reach enduring agreements?	−.29	**.51**	−.14	−.03	−.05	.08	.04	.14	−.13
25. To what extent did working with your team result in too many constraints (e.g., time/staff shortage, etc.) on this other team's everyday activities?	−.09	**.58**	−.16	.02	.07	.15	.07	.07	−.17
26. To what extent was there too much disagreement about resource allocation (e.g. time to invest, people or staff, allocation of tasks or duties, etc.) between your team and this other team?	−.23	**.70**	−.07	−.00	.03	−.00	.02	.06	−.13
27. To what extent did both teams work effectively together in order to respond to tasks or duties that emerged from working within the PCT (e.g., coordinating cross-team activities, assignment of organizational duties, etc.)?	.14	−.16	.08	−.00	−.07	.15	**−.48**	.19	.24
28. To what extent did you feel the relationship between your team and this other team was productive?*	.13	−.13	.08	−.08	.00	−.12	**−.59**	.04	.09

(continued overleaf)

TABLE 2
(continued)

	I	II	III	IV	V	VI	VII Resource exchange/system respon-siveness	VIII	IX
	Intergroup trust	Transaction costs	Team effectiveness	Forcing	Problem solving	Intergroup conflict		Viability	
29. To what extent did both teams work effectively together in order to provide better services to patients?	.15	.15	.09	.08	-.16	.03	**-.68**	-.00	.20
30. To what extent did both teams work effectively together in order to respond to problems or flaws that emerged from working within the PCT (e.g., staff or time shortage, etc.)?	-.13	.04	.06	-.07	.00	-.17	**-.68**	.00	-.11
31. To what extent did both teams effectively help each other out if resources (e.g., time to invest, people or staff, support, etc.) were needed?	-.03	-.03	-.04	.06	-.02	-.02	**-.80**	.01	.02
32. To what extent did both teams make effectively use of each other's resources (e.g., time to invest, people or staff, support, etc.) in order to provide better patient care?	.19	-.05	-.02	.00	-.00	.07	**-.77**	.04	-.05
33. To what extent did your team carry out your responsibilities and commitments in regard to this other team?*	-.04	.11	.07	-.01	-.06	-.03	.03	**.80**	.13
34. To what extent did this other team carry out its responsibilities and commitments in regard to your team?*	.12	-.12	-.03	-.01	-.03	-.04	-.38	**.54**	.04

$N = 158$; total variance explained: 68%; items loading above .40 in bold.
*Items from the Organizational Assessment Inventory (Van de Ven & Ferry, 1980).

automatically require the exchange of resources. Thus, our distinction between both scales may be more relevant from a theoretical than a practical point of view.

Group-level analysis

We chose Dawson's selection rate (2003) as a criterion to exclude teams with low team-level response rates from further analysis. Selection rate is a measure derived from Monte Carlo Simulations that assesses the accurateness of incomplete team-level data in predicting true scores as a function of team response rate and team size. The cutoff point chosen was a selection rate of .32, which suggests that scores measured by incomplete data are correlated with true scores to .95 or higher. Three teams were above this cutoff point and therefore deleted for further analysis, yielding a remaining sample of 51 teams.

Consensual and discriminable validity. We argued earlier that an intergroup theory would be justified as boundary spanners negotiate their group's interests, and not their personal interests, on behalf of their team. This suggests that all members within a team involved in cross-team working have similar perceptions on their relationships with other teams, and that these perceptions may vary across teams. Therefore we aggregated our intergroup effectiveness data for each team. Statistical justification of aggregating individuals' responses by groups is given if interrater agreement within teams is high, as measured by $r_{wg(j)}$ (George & James, 1993; James, Demaree, & Wolf, 1984). $R_{wg(j)}$ values above .70 suggest acceptable consensual validity (cf. Nunnally, 1978). Additionally, discriminant power needs to be assessed by demonstrating that the construct varies considerably across teams, suggesting that responses are dependent on team membership (see Yamarino & Markham, 1992). Thus, we computed one-way ANOVAs on the aggregated intergroup effectiveness subscales to calculate the intraclass coefficients ICC1 and ICC2. ICC2 values above .50 are suggestive of acceptable discriminant validity. Minimum evidence for differences across groups is indicated if an ICC1 index has F-ratios from an ANOVA greater than 1; however, researchers commonly use a significant F-ratio to justify aggregation (Klein et al., 2000a).

Table 3 illustrates that the average $r_{wg(j)}$ indices for the four subscales are above .70, indicating that all subscales have sufficient consensual validity. Controversial, however, is the measure's discriminable validity. With the exception of transaction costs, no subscale reaches the recommended ICC2 values of .50 or above. On the other hand, F-values of the ICC1 are above unity for all subscales, and significant for three of the subscales, suggesting that three of the four subscales have acceptable discriminant validity.

The literature discusses several potential reasons why indices of discriminant validity at group level yield inconsistent or low results. Firstly,

TABLE 3
Indices of consensual and discriminant validity

	$r_{wg(j)}$	ICC2	ICC1	F-value
System responsiveness	.84	.449	.119	1.81**
Resource exchange	.76	.381	.062	1.62*
Transaction costs	.86	.735	.228	3.77***
Viability	.84	.208	.027	1.26

$N = 51$ teams.
*$p < .05$; **$p < .01$; ***$p < .001$.

even though the ICC1 value controls for team size, the F-test for ICC1 indices and the ICC2 values are influenced by both number and size of the units in a sample. From there, the small size of our sample may have deteriorated results. Secondly, restrictions of range due to sample size artifacts can artificially cause low between group variance (George & James, 1993). Our teams are nested within a limited number of organizations, which are all embedded within the British National Health Service. They follow the same political and strategic guidelines, regulations, and have very similar organizational structures. Teams may therefore not vary indiscriminately with respect to our intergroup effectiveness construct.

Klein et al. (2000a) suggest that when indices lead to differing conclusions regarding aggregation, researchers may base their decision on theory, prior research, or the belief in the superior merits of one of the indices before aggregating their measures. Following the presented rationale in this article, we do consider aggregation theoretically justified, as issues dealt with at the interface between teams are interests relevant for groups as a whole, and not interpersonal issues (Brett & Rognes, 1986).

Consensual validity for both teams in a dyad

A critical issue in this research is that intergroup effectiveness is an intergroup construct, but information is gathered by only one team of each dyad. The implicit assumption that both teams of a dyad agree on their perceptions of the construct and therefore can be treated regarding their views on effectiveness as a homogenous whole is underlying this procedure. Klein, Palmer, and Buhl Conn (2000b) criticize this frequent problem in research with dyads and suggest an investigation into whether generalization is justified. We have therefore examined the four dyads within our sample in order to see whether both teams of the dyads agreed on their perceptions of intergroup effectiveness. Should both teams of a dyad rate intergroup effectiveness differently, the $r_{wg(j)}$ for the dyad as an entity should be substantially lower than the separate $r_{wg(j)}$ values for both individual teams.

TABLE 4
Comparison of $R_{wg(j)}$ values of teams individually and collapsed to dyads

	System responsiveness		Resource exchange		Transaction costs		Viability	
	$r_{wg(j)}$	$r_{wg(j)}$ dyad[ab]	$r_{wg(j)}$	$r_{wg(j)}$ dyad[ab]	$r_{wg(j)}$	$r_{wg(j)}$ dyad[ab]	$r_{wg(j)}$	$r_{wg(j)}$ dyad[ab]
Team 1[a]	.98		1.00		.85		.91	
		.94		.86		.89		.91
Team 1[b]	.92		.80		.89		.91	
Team 2[a]	.36		.50		.91		.96	
		.80		.75		.93		.85
Team 2[b]	.94		.93		.95		.93	
Team 3[a]	.98				.98		.86	
		.90		.79		.88		.00
Team 3[b]	.87		.80		.77		.00	
Team 4[a]	.97		.73		.89		.49	
		.94		.75		.89		.46
Team 4[b]	.76		.67		.84		.00	
Mean	.85	.89	.78	.79	.88	.90	.63	.55

$N = 8$ teams (4 dyads).

Table 4 displays the mean $r_{wg(j)}$ values for the intergroup effectiveness subscales for both teams of the dyads individually, and for entire dyads where we collapsed responses of both teams. Mean $r_{wg(j)}$ values for individual teams and entire dyads are very similar, with the biggest difference in $r_{wg(j)}$ for the viability subscale ($\Delta r_{wg(j)} = .08$). We therefore conclude that our (even though limited) data is suggestive of generalizing data from one team to the entire team dyad.

Internal homogeneity, intercorrelations, and predictive validity

Intercorrelations. Table 5 displays intercorrelations of study variables. Surprisingly, and contrary to expectations derived from SIT, team effectiveness, and intergroup conflict are negatively correlated, $r = -.36$, $p < .01$, indicating that more effective teams also develop less conflict with other teams. Such a carryover effect was previously found in experimental research, where student groups that previously cooperated internally were also more cooperative in subsequent between group negotiations, whilst groups that experienced internal conflict were more competitive in subsequent between group negotiations, relative to a control condition (Keenan & Carnevale, 1989). The consistently lower correlations between predictor variables and externally rated intergroup

TABLE 5
Intercorrelations among study variables at group level

	α	M	SD	1.	2.	3.	4.	5.	6.	7.	8.	9.	10.	11.	12.	13.
1. Intergroup trust	.87	3.63	0.53	1	−.81** (51)	−.10 (51)	.43** (51)	.42** (51)	−.74** (51)	.39** (51)	.68** (51)	.19 (37)	.36* (33)	.76** (51)	.13 (37)	.36* (33)
2. Intergroup conflict	.81	2.23	0.53	—	1	.15 (51)	−.37** (51)	−.36** (51)	.53** (51)	−.33* (51)	−.58** (51)	−.20 (37)	−.33§ (33)	−.52** (51)	−.17 (37)	−.43* (33)
3. Forcing	.63	1.90	0.42	—	—	1	−.02 (51)	−.07 (51)	−.09 (51)	.08 (51)	.03 (51)	−.02 (37)	.19 (33)	−.06 (51)	−.21 (37)	−.02 (33)
4. Problem solving	.69	3.70	0.39	—	—	—	1	.06 (51)	−.20 (51)	.39** (51)	.46** (51)	.11 (37)	.16 (33)	.46** (51)	.18 (37)	.22 (33)
5. Team effectiveness	.87	3.84	0.38	—	—	—	—	1	−.28* (51)	.32* (51)	.42** (51)	.31§ (37)	.16 (33)	.42** (51)	.14 (37)	.10 (33)
6. Transaction costs	.81	2.22	0.62	−.53** (50)	.42* (51)	.02 (49)	.00 (49)	−.22 (51)	1	−.34* (51)	−.52** (51)	−.29§ (37)	−.24 (33)	−.55** (51)	−.13 (37)	−.37* (33)
7. Viability	.76	3.33	0.49	.21 (50)	−.26§ (51)	.12 (49)	.19 (49)	.25§ (51)	−.36** (51)	1	.64** (51)	.33* (37)	.41* (33)	.46** (51)	.28§ (37)	.40* (33)
8. System responsiveness (self)	.82	3.34	0.49	.33* (49)	−.31 (50)	.10 (48)	−.01 (48)	.33* (50)	−.49** (50)	.56** (50)	1	.32§ (37)	.47** (33)	.81** (51)	.25 (37)	.43* (33)
9. System responsiveness (external) T1	.93	3.15	0.84	—	—	—	—	—	—	—	—	1	.62** (33)	.44 (37)	.86** (37)	.60** (33)
10. System responsiveness (external) T2	.81	3.38	0.58	—	—	—	—	—	—	—	—	—	1	.45** (33)	.50** (33)	.70** (33)
11. Resource exchange (self)	.84	3.31	0.59	.32* (49)	−.35* (50)	.02 (48)	−.06 (48)	.34* (50)	−.44** (50)	.43** (50)	.80** (50)	—	—	1	.36* (37)	.50** (33)
12. Resource exchange (external) T1	.90	3.08	1.04	—	—	—	—	—	—	—	—	—	—	—	1	.58** (33)
13. Resource exchange (external) T2	.78	3.17	0.81	—	—	—	—	—	—	—	—	—	—	—	—	1

Full sample correlations are above the diagonal of autocorrelations; split sample correlations are below the diagonal

N in parentheses.

§$p < .10$; *$p < .05$; **$p < .01$.

196

effectiveness in comparison to self-rated intergroup effectiveness indicates that correlations may be inflated due to common method variance. Especially the very high correlations of transaction costs with intergroup conflict and intergroup trust, $r = .74$ and $.53$, $ps < .01$, respectively, may question the constructs' discriminant validity. In order to correct these correlations from biases (e.g., hypothesis guessing and cognitive consistency effects), we controlled for common source variance (cf. Beersma & De Dreu, 1999). We randomly split individuals of each team in alternating order into two groups and subsequently aggregated responses from both groups per team. Then we correlated responses from both groups across all teams. These split sample correlations with self-report data on intergroup effectiveness are displayed below the diagonal in Table 5. The correlation between transaction costs and intergroup trust were then reduced to $-.53$ ($p < .01$), and between transaction costs and intergroup conflict to $.42$ ($p < .05$), providing further evidence for the discriminant power of the intergroup effectiveness scale.

Internal homogeneity. Table 5 shows that Cronbach's alphas are acceptable to good, ranging from .76 (viability) to .93 (externally rated system responsiveness), suggesting that our subscales have acceptable to good internal consistencies. Self and external ratings of intergroup effectiveness at T1 are moderately positive correlated, r resource exchange self and external $= .36$, $p < .05$; r system responsiveness self and external $= .32$, $p < .10$, providing further evidence for the construct's consensual validity. As expected, the four intergroup effectiveness subscales are mostly significantly intercorrelated, suggesting a superordinate factor of intergroup effectiveness.

Predictive validity. Table 5 also contains line managers' effectiveness ratings at T2, 5 months after the questionnaire was disseminated and the first effectiveness ratings were obtained. The best predictor of intergroup effectiveness was intergroup conflict, r conflict and system responsiveness T2 $= -.33$, $p < .10$; r conflict and resource exchange T2 $= -.43$, $p < .05$, suggesting the measure to be a suitable alternative outcome criterion of intergroup conflict.

DISCUSSION

We argued in this article that existing criteria describing effective intergroup relations are deficient. In particular, we disagreed that the absence or successful management of intergroup conflict would suffice to describe effective intergroup relations. Instead, we postulated that effective intergroup relations can best be described by four alternative outcome criteria conceptually unrelated to intergroup conflict and alternative constructs. We examined the psychometric properties of a scale measuring these criteria. The psychometric properties supported its validity and reliability in most aspects. Support for the four-factor structure was controversial. We clearly identified and separated two of the hypothesized factors, transaction costs and viability, with CFA, exploratory factor analysis, and intercorrelational analysis. CFA suggested that the four-factor model fits the data very well. However, both exploratory factor analysis and correlational analysis yielded that two of the subscales, system responsiveness and resource exchange, may represent a single factor measuring intergroup productivity. Consensual validity was supported by high $r_{wg(j)}$ values, moderately positive correlations of self with external ratings, and high interrater agreements of a subsample of four team dyads. Support for discriminant validity was controversial. Factor analysis using individual-level data clearly distinguished intergroup effectiveness from measures of team effectiveness, intergroup conflict, intergroup behaviour, and intergroup attitude. Similarly, correlational analysis at team level showed that, even though intergroup effectiveness subscales were correlated with other scales, intergroup effectiveness remained a distinct construct. Group-level analysis, however, yielded mixed results. Greater variation between than within teams for all four subscales suggests that the construct has discriminable validity across groups. ICC1 and ICC2 indices, however, led to different conclusions whether discriminable validity for two of the four subscales was sufficient to justify aggregation of data at group level. In the case of viability, both indicators concord that discriminant validity across teams, even though exceeding within group variability, is very low. We discussed how sample characteristics, in particular that the teams are nested within a limited sample of very similar organizations, might have caused such a restriction in variance across teams. Both intergroup conflict and intergroup trust were the most significant predictors of line managers' ratings of intergroup effectiveness at T2.

Overall, we presented a theory-driven, short, but parsimonious measure of intergroup effectiveness. Among its strengths is certainly its clear demarcation from related constructs, as well as its (with the exception of discriminable validity at group level) acceptable to very good psychometric properties. Its independence from intergroup conflict in particular indicates how little is known so far about the concept of intergroup effectiveness. Future studies may investigate whether a three- or four-factor solution represents the construct best, and whether the same factors are distinguishable with samples comprising groups from a diverse range of organizations. Also, the measure is of great utility for organizational research, as it is short and can easily be administered within a larger survey.

The construct of intergroup effectiveness represents an alternative outcome of organizational conflict, hitherto ignored by conflict researchers, which is built upon boundary spanners' and line managers' subjective value judgements of effective cross-group working. The disruptive effects of intergroup conflict on aspects of intergroup effectiveness have been indicated and discussed, but not properly measured (e.g., Lawrence & Lorsch, 1967a, 1967b). Of particular interest may be under which conditions intergroup conflict positively predicts intergroup effectiveness. Intergroup conflict, in contrast to intragroup conflict, has predominantly been seen as detrimental for organizations, with a few exceptions focusing on beneficial aspects as well (see Dutton & Walton, 1969; Erev, Bornstein, & Galilei, 1993; Putnam, 1997). As we provided evidence for a measure that is conceptually different from intergroup conflict, it is now possible to investigate the effects of intergroup conflict on intergroup effectiveness, as well as potential moderators of this relationship. Similarly, the effect of within-group conflict on intergroup effectiveness may be examined within the SIT or alternative frameworks, like the carryover effect (Keenan & Carnevale, 1989).

REFERENCES

Aiken, M., & Hage, J. (1968). Organizational independence and intraorganizational structure. *American Sociological Review, 33*(9), 912–930.

Alderfer, C. P. (1986). An intergroup perspective on group dynamics. In J. Lorsch (Ed.), *Handbook of organizational behavior.* Englewood Cliffs, NJ: Prentice-Hall.

Allport, G. W. (1954). *The nature of prejudice.* Reading, MA: Addison-Wesley.

Arbuckle, J. L. (1995). *AMOS 3.5 for Windows.* Chicago: Small Waters Corporation.

Beersma, B., & De Dreu, C. K. W. (1999). Negotiation processes and outcomes in prosocially and egoistically motivated groups. *International Journal of Conflict Management, 10*(4), 385–402.

Blake, R. R., Sheppard, H. A., & Mouton, J. S. (1966). *Managing intergroup conflict in industry.* Houston, TX: Gulf Publishing Company.

Brett, J. M., & Rognes, J. K. (1986). Intergroup relations in organizations. In P. S. Goodman & Associates (Eds.), *Designing effective work groups.* San Francisco: Jossey-Bass Publishers.

Brewer, M. B., & Brown, R. J. (1998). Intergroup relations. In D. T. Gilbert & S. T. Fiske (Eds.), *The handbook of social psychology* (4th ed., Vol. 2, pp. 554–594). New York: McGraw-Hill.

Cummings, L. L., & Bromiley, P. (1996). The Organizational Trust Inventory: Development and validation. In R. M. Kramer & T. R. Tyler (Eds.), *Trust in organizations: Frontiers of theory and research.* Thousand Oaks, CA: Sage.

Dawson, J. F. (2003). *Do we have enough? The accuracy of incomplete data from small groups.* Paper presented at the conference of the Academy of Management, Seattle, WA, USA.

De Dreu, C. K. W., Evers, A., Beersma, B., Kluwer, E. S., & Nauta, A. (2001). A theory-based measure of conflict management strategies in the workplace. *Journal of Organizational Behavior, 22*, 645–668.

De Dreu, C. K. W., Harinck, F., & Van Vianen, A. E. M. (1999). Conflict and performance in groups and organizations. In C. L. Cooper & I. T. Robertson (Eds.), *International review of industrial and organizational psychology* (Vol. 14, pp. 376–405). Chichester, UK: Wiley.

Deutsch, M. (1973). *The resolution of conflict: Constructive and destructive processes.* New Haven, CT: Yale University Press.

Dutton, J. M., & Walton, R. E. (1966). Interdepartmental conflict and cooperation: Two contrasting studies. *Human Organizations, 25,* 207–220.

Erev, I., Bornstein, G., & Galilei, R. (1993). Constructive intergroup competition as a solution to the free rider problem: A field experiment. *Journal of Experimental Social Psychology, 29,* 463–476.

Festinger, L. (1954). A theory of social comparison processes. *Human Relations, 7,* 117–140.

Gaertner, S. L., Dovidio, J. F., Rust, M. C., Nier, J. A., Banker, B. S., Ward, C. M., Mottola, G. R., & Houlette, M. (1999). Reducing intergroup bias: Elements of intergroup cooperation. *Journal of Personality and Social Psychology, 76*(3), 388–402.

George, J. M., & James, L. R. (1993). Personality, affect, and behavior in groups revisited: Comment on aggregation, levels of analysis, and a recent application of within and between analysis. *Journal of Applied Psychology, 78*(5), 798–804.

Gerbing, D. W., & Anderson, J. C. (1993). Monte Carlo evaluations of goodness-of-fit for structural equation models. In K. A. Bollen & J. S. Long (Eds.), *Testing structural equation models* (pp. 40–65). Newbury Park, CA: Sage.

Gladstein, D. L. (1984). Groups in context: A model and task group effectiveness. *Administrative Science Quarterly, 29,* 499–517.

Hackman, J. R. (1987). The design of work teams. In J. W. Lorsch (Ed.), *Handbook of organizational behavior* (pp. 315–342). Englewood Cliffs, NJ: Prentice-Hall.

Hartley, J. F. (1996). Intergroup relations in organizations. In M. A. West (Ed.), *Handbook of work group psychology.* Chichester, UK: Wiley.

Haslam, A. (2001). The social identity approach. In A. Haslam (Ed.), *Psychology in organizations: The social identity approach.* London: Sage.

James, L. R., Demaree, R. G., & Wolf, G. (1984). Estimating within-group interrater reliability with and without response bias. *Journal of Applied Psychology, 69,* 85–89.

Jones, J. (1997). Team performance measurement: Theoretical and applied issues. *Advances in Interdisciplinary Studies of Work Teams, 4,* 115–139.

Keenan, P. A., & Carnevale, P. J. (1989). Positive effects of within-group cooperation on between-group negotiation. *Journal of Applied Social Psychology, 19*(12), 977–992.

Klein, K. J., Bliese, P. D., Kozlowski, S. W. J., Dansereau, F., Gavin, M. B., Griffin, M. A., Hofmann, D. A., James, L. R., Yammarino, F. J., & Bligh, M. C. (2000a). Multilevel perspective. In K. J. Klein & S. W. J. Kozlowski (Eds.), *Multilevel theory, research, and methods in organizations* (pp. 512–556). San Francisco: Jossey-Bass.

Klein, K. J., Conn, A. B., Smith, D. B., & Sorra, J. S. (2001). Is everyone in agreement? An exploration of within-group agreement in employee perceptions of the work environment. *Journal of Applied Psychology, 86*(1), 3–16.

Klein, K. J., Palmer, S. L., & Buhl Conn, A. (2000b). Interorganizational relationships: A multilevel perspective. In K. J. Klein & S. W. J. Kozlowski (Eds.), *Multilevel theory, research, and methods in organizations* (pp. 267–307). San Francisco: Jossey-Bass.

Lawrence, P. R., & Lorsch, J. W. (1967a). Differentiation and integration in complex organizations. *Administrative Science Quarterly, 10,* 21–38.

Lawrence, P. R., & Lorsch, J. W. (1967b). *Organization and environment: Managing differentiation and integration.* Boston: Harvard Graduate School of Business Administration.

Marsh, H. W., Balla, J. R., & Hau, K. T. (1996). An evaluation of incremental fit indices: A clarification of mathematical and empirical properties. In G. A. Marcoulides & R. E. Schumacker (Eds.), *Advanced structural equation modelling: Issues and techniques.* Mahwah, NJ: Lawrence Erlbaum Associates, Inc.

Mathieu, J. E., Marks, M. A., & Zaccaro, S. J. (2001). Multiteam systems. In N. Anderson, D. S. Ones, H. K. Sinangil, & C. Viswesvaran (Eds.), *Handbook of industrial, work, and organizational psychology* (pp. 289 – 313). London: Sage.

McCann, J., & Galbraith, J. R. (1981). Interdepartmental relations. In P. C. Nystrom & W. H. Starbuck (Eds.), *Handbook of organizational design.* New York: Oxford University Press.

Mohrmann, S. A., Cohen, S. G., & Mohrmann, A. M. (1995). *Designing team-based organizations: New forms for knowledge work.* San Francisco: Jossey-Bass.

Nauta, A., & Sanders, K. (2000). Interdepartmental negotiation behavior in manufacturing organizations. *International Journal of Conflict Management, 11*(2), 135 – 161.

Nunnally, J. C. (1978). *Psychometric theory.* New York: McGraw-Hill.

Putnam, L. L. (1997). Productive conflict: Negotiation as implicit coordination. In C. K. W. de Dreu & E. van de Vliert (Eds.), *Using conflict in organizations* (pp. 147 – 160). London: Sage.

Rahim, M. A. (2001). *Managing conflict in organizations.* San Francisco: Quorum Books.

Richter, A., Van Dick, R., & West, M. A. (2004). The relationship between group and organizational identification and effective intergroup relations. *Best Paper Proceedings of the Annual Meeting of the Academy of Management, New Orleans, USA.*

Schopler, J., Insko, C. A., Wieselquist, J., Pemberton, M., Witcher, B., Kozar, R., Roddenberry, C., & Wildschut, T. (2001). When groups are more competitive than individuals: The domain of the discontinuity effect. *Journal of Personality and Social Psychology, 80*(4), 632 – 644.

Sherif, M. (1966). *Group conflict and cooperation.* London: Routledge & Kegan Paul.

Tajfel, H. (1978). *Differentiation between social groups: Studies in the social psychology of intergroup relations.* Oxford, UK: Academic Press.

Tajfel, H., & Turner, J. C. (1979). An integrative theory of intergroup conflict relations. In W. G. Austin & S. Worchel (Eds.), *The social psychology of intergroup relations* (pp. 33 – 47). Monterey, CA: Brooks/Cole.

Terry, D. J., & Callan, V. J. (1998). Ingroup bias in response to an organizational merger. *Group Dynamics: Theory, Research, and Practice, 2*(2), 67 – 81.

Thomas, K. W. (1992). Conflict and negotiation processes in organizations. In M. D. Dunette & L. M. Hough (Eds.), *Handbook of industrial and organizational psychology* (2nd ed., Vol. 3, pp. 651 – 717). Chicago: Rand-McNally.

Tjosvold, D. (1988). Cooperative and competitive interdependence: Collaboration between departments to serve customers. *Group and Organization Studies, 13*(3), 274 – 289.

Tjosvold, D. (1991). Forging synergy. In D. Tjosvold (Ed.), *Team organisation: An enduring competitive advantage* (pp. 219 – 233). Chichester, UK: Wiley.

Tjosvold, D. (1998). Co-operative and competitive goal approaches to conflict: Accomplishments and challenges. *Applied Psychology: An International Review, 47,* 285 – 342.

Tjosvold, D., Dann, V., & Wong, C. (1992). Managing conflict between departments to serve customers. *Human Relations, 45,* 1035 – 1054.

Van de Ven, A., & Ferry, D. (1980). *Measuring and assessing organizations.* New York: Wiley & Sons.

Van Knippenberg, D. (2003). Intergroup relations in organizations. In M. A. West, D. Tjosvold, & K. G. Smith (Eds.), *International handbook of organizational teamwork and cooperative working* (pp. 381 – 400). Chichester, UK: Wiley.

Vinokur-Kaplan, D. (1995). Treatment teams that work (and those that don't): An application of Hackman's group effectiveness model to interdisciplinary teams in psychiatric hospitals. *Journal of Applied Behavioral Science, 31*(3), 303 – 327.

Walton, R. E. (1966). Theory of conflict in lateral relationships. In J. R. Lawrence (Ed.), *Operational research and the social sciences* (pp. 409 – 428). London: Tavistock.

Walton, R. E., & Dutton, J. M. (1969). The management of interdepartmental conflict: A model and review. *Administrative Science Quarterly, 14,* 73 – 84.

Wildschut, T., Pinter, B., Vevea, J. L., Insko, C. A., & Schopler, J. (2003). Beyond the group mind: A quantitative review of the interindividual–intergroup discontinuity effect. *Journal of Personality and Social Psychology, 129*(5), 698–722.

Williamson, O. E. (1975). *Markets and hierarchies: Analysis and antitrust implications.* New York: Free Press.

Yamarino, F. J., & Markham, S. E. (1992). On the application of within and between analysis: Are absence and affect really group-based phenomena? *Journal of Applied Psychology, 77,*168–176.

APPENDIX
The Intergroup Effectiveness Scale

Criterion 1: System responsiveness

- To what extent did both teams work effectively together in order to respond to *tasks or duties that emerged from working within the Trust* (e.g., coordinating cross-team activities, assignment of organizational duties, etc.)?
- To what extent did both teams *work effectively together* in order to provide better services to patients?
- To what extent did you feel the *relationship* between your team and this other team was *productive*?*
- To what extent did both teams work effectively together in order to respond to *problems or flaws that emerged from working within the Trust* (e.g., staff or time shortage, etc.)?

Criterion 2: Resource exchange

- For *this other team* to accomplish its goals and responsibilities, to what extent did it receive the expected services, resources, or support from your team?
- For *your team* to accomplish its goals and responsibilities, to what extent did you receive the expected services, resources, or support from this other team?
- To what extent did both teams effectively *help each other out* if resources (e.g., time to invest, people or staff, support, etc.) were needed?
- To what extent did both teams *make effectively use of each other's resources* (e.g., time to invest, people or staff, support, etc.) in order to provide better patient care?

Criterion 3: Transaction costs

- To what extent did working with this other team result in *too many constraints* (e.g., time/staff shortage, etc.) for your team's everyday activities?
- To what extent did working with your team result in *too many constraints* (e.g., time/staff shortage, etc.) for this other team's everyday activities?
- To what extent did working with this other team entail *too much loss of time and energy* on trying to reach *enduring agreements*?
- To what extent was there *too much disagreement about resource allocation* (e.g., time to invest, people or staff, allocation of tasks or duties, etc.) between your team and this other team?

(*continued overleaf*)

Criterion 4: Viability

- To what extent did *your team* carry out your responsibilities and commitments in regard to this other team?*
- To what extent did *this other team* carry out its responsibilities and commitments in regard to your team?*
- If you consider the *fairness* of the give-and-take relationship with this team, to what extent did you feel that *this other team* should have given more than it did?*
- If you consider the *fairness* of the give-and-take relationship with this other team, to what extent did you feel that *your team* should have given more than it did?*

Items were answered on a 1–5 Likert scale (1 = "to no extent", to 5 = "great extent").
Items were presented in random order and in two different questionnaire versions.
*Items from the Organizational Assessment Inventory (Van de Ven & Ferry, 1980).

Call for Papers

Authors are invited to submit a paper for a special issue of the *European Journal of Work and Organizational Psychology* on:

Psychological and organizational climate research from different cultural perspectives

Differences in culture (e.g., focusing on individuals versus collectives) and research traditions have cultivated different ways of looking at work climate. For instance, the quantitative Anglo-American approach tends to focus on the measurement of specific climate dimensions at the individual-level of analysis (i.e., psychological climate), and the employment of composition arguments and assessments of interrater agreement for studying climate at the organization-level of analysis. This focus is in contrast to climate research in some European countries, which is characterized as a more phenomenologically oriented approach to global assessments of climate at the organization-level of analysis. Cultural differences impact not only the content and nature of climate measures, but also may influence the types of criteria that are focused on in relation to what workers value versus what work organization's value.

The purpose of this special issue is to publish original research on work climate from different cultural perspectives and research traditions. The articles selected for the special issue will illustrate how climate research within different countries and cultures is both different and complementary, and offer progress toward advancing research and practice on work climate. Contributions dealing with all aspects or research on work climate will be considered. Authors are asked to pay particular attention to how climate and its antecedents and consequences are conceptualized and measured at the individual or organizational levels of analysis, and what are the implications of the research findings for future research and professional practice.

The special issue will be guest edited by Alessia D'Amato (University of Surrey) and Michael Burke (Tulane University). Questions concerning possible submissions from countries within the European Union can be directed to Alessia D'Amato (*a.damato@surrey.ac.uk*) and from outside the European Union to Michael Burke (*mburke1@tulane.edu*).

Manuscripts should be prepared following the guidelines in the APA Publication Manual (5th ed.). Please email your manuscript in a standard document format such as Word, Rich Text Format, or PDF to: *reviews@psypress.co.uk*

All submissions will be peer reviewed.

Manuscripts are to be submitted by October 31, 2005.

For Product Safety Concerns and Information please contact our EU
representative GPSR@taylorandfrancis.com Taylor & Francis Verlag GmbH,
Kaufingerstraße 24, 80331 München, Germany

Batch number: 08153778

Printed by Printforce, the Netherlands